HUDSON TAYLOR

J. Hudson Taylor.

HUDSON TAYLOR

The Man who believed God

BY

MARSHALL BROOMHALL, M.A.

Εχετε πίσιν Θεου
—Mark 11:22

SCRIPTURE TESTIMONY EDITION

WALKING TOGETHER PRESS
ESTES PARK · JENTA MANGORO

© 2023 Walking Together Press

Published in 2023 by
Walking Together Press
Estes Park, Colorado USA
Jenta Mangoro, Jos, Plateau Nigeria
https://walkingtogether.life

ISBN: 978-1-961568-06-8

Hudson Taylor: The Man Who Believed God is in the public domain
Text and images from the 1929 edition published by China Inland Mission, Philadelphia

Cover design by D. Thaine Norris
Typeset in Adobe Garamond Pro by D. Thaine Norris

1

ABOUT THE SCRIPTURE TESTIMONY EDITION

HUDSON TAYLOR was as a nineteenth century missionary to China and founder of the China Inland Mission. He did these things by faith, trusting only God for all temporal supplies for himself, his family, and more than eight hundred missionaries that joined him in more than fifty years of Gospel labor. While these are impressive numbers, Hudson Taylor was first and foremost a child of God, constantly growing in his faith. One of Taylor's greatest gifts to posterity is the transparency with which he wrote about life challenges and his own faith journey. This book contains story after real-life story of walking ever more closely with God, each demonstrating His reality and the truth of His Word.

The *Scripture Testimony Index* is an extensive research project by Walking Together Press to use artificial intelligence and data science to develop a New-Testament-driven subject index across a large body of missionary biographies and personal narratives. In analyzing the database of these books programmatically; beautiful, bright threads emerge, threads of prayer, provision, deliverance, specific leading, healing, transformation, and miraculous salvation. The end result is an index of short story excerpts organized by subject and Scripture verse that empirically demonstrate the truth of the Scriptures, and which is freely available on our website at https://walkingtogether.life.

Walking Together Press has enhanced this classic title, *Hudson Taylor: The Man Who Believed God*, by identifying and marking thirty-five portions of the narrative that illustrate specific Biblical topics and verses. An extensive *Scripture Testimony Index* has also been added containing short summaries of how each Scriptural topic is illustrated, making locating specific stories easy. Furthermore, this title is one of many in the *Scripture Testimony Collection.*

TO
HOWARD AND GERALDINE TAYLOR
BY THEIR
COUSIN AND DEBTOR

Blessed is the man whose strength is in Thee.
Psalm 84:5

FOREWORD

IN THE years 1911 and 1918, respectively, the two volumes, *Hudson Taylor in Early Years,* and *Hudson Taylor and the China Inland Mission,* were published. Both were written by Dr. and Mrs. Howard Taylor, and both have had a remarkable circulation. Up to the time of writing nearly 50,000 volumes have been sold, and many are the tokens that these books have brought much blessing to the readers.

But these two volumes together aggregate nearly 1200 closely printed demy octavo pages, and it has been long evident that a shorter Life, in one small volume, was needed. More than one publishing house has contemplated the issue of such a biography, and several of these have kindly relinquished the idea of issuing the same, that the book might be published by the China Inland Mission itself. Grateful acknowledgement of this courtesy is hereby made.

It had been hoped that Dr. and Mrs. Howard Taylor, the authors of the authoritative work mentioned above, might have undertaken this smaller volume also; but that was not found possible. The one to whom this task eventually fell desires to make full acknowledgement of the immeasurable help obtained from the larger Life. At the same time, it may be mentioned, original sources have not been neglected. The writer is also most thankful to state that his cousin, Dr. Howard Taylor, has read and criticized, with his accustomed care, the whole of the manuscript before it went to the printer. It is therefore with more confidence that the book is issued to the public, though the writer accepts the final responsibility for the volume as it stands.

An endeavour has been made to present this shorter Life from a somewhat different angle than the larger work. It is divided into three parts; the first, dealing with Hudson Taylor's Birth and Call; the second, referring to his early years of missionary service, prior to the formation of the China Inland Mission; and the third, dealing with his life as Founder and Leader of that Mission.

In the first two sections the story has been told in a straightforward chronological order; but in the third and last section, which occupies nearly one half of the volume, a different method has been adopted. That this small book might be exclusively a study of the man, and that space might be saved by abstaining from retelling the story of the China Inland Mission—a story already told more than once—the strictly chronological order has given way to a study of character, as revealed by outstanding acts, significant writings, unique methods, and other distinctive features. In all this a chronological sequence has been followed, so far as that was possible, but in a subservient manner. The object aimed at has been to reveal the man himself, and the secret of his success as a leader of men, and as a master-builder in God's work. To correct any loss that this method might entail, a detailed chronological summary has been given a place in an appendix. This summary will enable the reader, at a glance, to trace Mr. Taylor's movements from place to place, and from year to year.

In the study of Hudson Taylor's character the student is greatly assisted by a life particularly rich in action and decisive deeds. "A great act," said the late Professor J. B. Mosley, in his *Lectures on the Old Testament,* "gathers up and brings to a focus the whole habit and general character of the man. The act is dramatic.

...There is a boundlessness in an act. It is not a divided, balanced thing, but is like an immense spring or leap. The whole of the man is in it, and at one great stroke is revealed.... Single acts are treasures. They are like new ideas in the people's minds. There is something in them which moulds, which lifts up to another level, and gives an impulse to human nature. If we examine any one of those signal acts which are historical, we shall find that they could none of them have been done but for one great idea with which the person was possessed, or to which he had attached himself."

There can be no doubt but that Hudson Taylor's acts have helped to mould men's minds, and have given an impulse to missionary activity and methods. They have had an educational value of far-reaching import, and have fructified and reproduced themselves.

And there can be no question as to the great idea with which he was possessed, and to which he attached himself. His life was dominated from first to last by his conviction as to the utter faithfulness of God. It is for this reason that the title of this little book has been called: *Hudson Taylor: The Man who believed God.*

MARSHALL BROOMHALL.
Midsummer-day, 1929.

CONTENTS

PART III
THE MISSIONARY LEADER
1865-1905 · AET. 33-73

HUDSON TAYLOR

PART I

1832-1853
BIRTH AND CALL
AET. 1-21

A SERVANT OF JESUS CHRIST
CALLED TO BE AN APOSTLE
SEPARATED UNTO THE GOSPEL OF GOD
Romans 1:1

I

THE MAN WHO BELIEVED GOD

"**I**F HUDSON Taylor had not been a missionary," wrote a distinguished editor some time after Hudson Taylor's death. "If Hudson Taylor had been a statesman, for example, there is no doubt whatever, that he would have been reckoned one of the few greatest British statesmen of our time.... If he had gone out to China with money and enterprise and had succeeded in covering that vast land with British traders, as he did cover it with British evangelists, his name would have been as familiar to the man in the street as the name of Strathcona or Cecil Rhodes. And yet his influence in China, and through China on the world, will be greater than either of these two men, and an influence, moreover, that is altogether good."

This is a large claim, and some may be disposed to challenge it; but it may be allowed to stand as an illustration of the impression made upon the mind of one not incompetent observer.

"The power inherent in a simple faith, without any accessories or system, remains an awe-inspiring and tremendous fact," wrote Bishop Parker, the Secretary of the Society for the Propagation of the Gospel, a day or two after Hudson Taylor's death "We can be thankful," he continued, "for the one deep lesson taught to this generation by the founder of the China Inland Mission, the power of the pure flame of a passionate belief. There is nothing quite like it in the world, and from it have come the great miracles of action in history.... The spiritual force has been so great that no Church or denomination can show so imposing a mass of missionary agents in China as the Inland Mission, with the exception of the Church of Rome, with its four centuries of work behind it."

And Dr. Eugene Stock, Secretary of the Church Missionary Society, when speaking at Hudson Taylor's memorial service in London, said: "I have been thinking of various great missionary pioneers, and I have tried to think which of them our dear friend was like. I have thought of John Eliot and Hans Egede. I have thought of Ziegenbalg, and Carey, and Duff; Morrison, and William Burns, and Gilmour. I have thought of John Williams, and Samuel Marsden, and Patteson, and Allen Gardiner. I have thought of Moffat, and Krapf, and Livingstone; great men, indeed, some of them, as the world would say, much greater than our dear friend. But I do not find among them one exactly like him, and I am much mistaken if we shall not in the course of years, if the Lord tarry, begin to see that Hudson Taylor was sanctioned, enabled, and permitted by the Lord to do a work, not less than any of them, if indeed, one might not say, greater in some respects."

These are great testimonies from men well qualified to speak. And the secret of it all was Hudson Taylor's simple, childlike, unshakable faith in God. He is simply inconceivable apart from his faith in the Word, and Character, of God. There is no other explanation of the man. What he was, and what he did, sprang from no other root, had no other origin. God's character was his only confidence; God's Word was the sole foundation for his feet. These were the eternal truths which inspired him; these were the secret of his strength, the reason and justification of his enterprise, the ground of his convictions, the fount of his joy, and the rock on which he built. If there is one Scripture, more than another, inseparably associated with his name, it is: "Have faith in God." In God he literally lived, moved, and had his being. It was this that exalted the whole man, and added force to every faculty. It enlarged his heart toward all the world, and especially toward China. He knew God, was strong, and did exploits.

"Oh for the clear accent, the ringing, joyous note of apostolic assurance!" wrote one who is now beyond the veil. "We want a faith not loud, but deep; a faith not born of sentiment and human sympathy, but that comes from the vision of the Living God." It was this that Hudson Taylor possessed. It was this that he enjoyed. He believed God.

II

FACE TO FACE WITH GOD

IT IS a memorable moment in the life of any man when he is first brought face to face with God. Such an event is only comparable to birth itself, for a man is then begotten again unto a new and living experience. It was so with Moses when he drew near with uncovered feet to the burning bush. It was so with Isaiah when, in the year that King Uzziah died, he saw the Lord. It was so with Saul when he met Christ outside the walls of Damascus. That encounter changed his name, his character, his ambitions, his all. Henceforth the Apostle Paul was a new creature, old things had passed away, all things had become new. And so it was with Hudson Taylor.

Of that never-to-be-forgotten experience Hudson Taylor wrote in after life as follows:

"Not many months after my conversion, having a leisure afternoon, I retired to my own chamber to spend it largely in communion with

SCRIPTURE TESTIMONY
We must believe that God exists and that He rewards those who seek Him
MATTHEW 6:6 · HEBREWS 11:6

God. Well do I remember that occasion, how in gladness of my heart I poured out my soul before God; and again and again confessing my grateful love to Him who had done everything for me—who had saved me when I had given up all hope and even desire for salvation—I besought Him to give me some work to do for Him, as an outlet for love and gratitude, some self-denying service, no matter what it might be, however trying or however trivial; something with which He would be pleased, and that I might do for Him who had done so much for me!

"Well do I remember, as in unreserved consecration I put myself, my life, my friends, my all, upon the altar, the deep solemnity that came over my soul with the assurance that my offering was accepted. The presence of God became unutterably real and blessed; and though only a child under sixteen,[1] I remember stretching myself on the ground, and lying there silent before Him with unspeakable awe and unspeakable joy.

"For what service I was accepted I knew not; but a deep consciousness that I was no longer my own took possession of me, which has never since been effaced. It has been a very practical consciousness."

That private chamber in that humble home in Barnsley, Yorkshire, became to Hudson Taylor another Peniel; for had he not, as Jacob of old, seen God face to face. Henceforth, in his degree, he was to be another prince with God, and by his prayers and faith prevail.

This deep sense of God was followed not long afterward by an overwhelming assurance of a Divine vocation. It was as though he heard the voice of God Himself saying to his inmost soul: "Then go for Me to China." This solemn and momentous experience he briefly alluded to in a letter addressed to a friend in London in the following words:

"Never shall I forget the feeling that came over me then. Words can never describe it. I felt that I was in the very presence of God, entering into a covenant with the Almighty. I felt as though I wished to withdraw my promise, but could not. Something

---

1   This was written by Mr. Taylor from memory in 1894, forty-five years after the event. It should correctly read "under eighteen." See his own letter dated April 25, 1851, written a little more than a year after the experience itself, and printed in full in *Hudson Taylor in Early Years*, pp. 101-104.

seemed to say: 'Your prayer is answered, your conditions are accepted.' And from that time the conviction has never left me that I was called to China.'

"From that hour," to quote his mother's words, "his mind was made up. His pursuits and studies were all engaged in with reference to this object, and whatever difficulties presented themselves his purpose never wavered."

In these two outstanding experiences lay, in large measure, the secret of the life which followed. In one way or another all God's prophets have received, as their preparation for their life's work, first the vision of God Himself, and then the sense of call. Thus, and thus only, can a man be qualified for any task which surpasses human powers. It is from such an audience with the King of kings, and from the commission then received, that the power for a life of exacting service, and maybe of suffering and death, proceeds. To understand the life of Hudson Taylor aright these early and all-important experiences must be fully appreciated. They were crucial. They were the inspiration of every subsequent enterprise, and the ground of his unaltered and unshaken confidence.

But these initial experiences, though vital, were but the beginning of an ever-deepening and extending knowledge of God which accompanied and followed every fresh adventure of faith. None the less, these early realizations of God, and of God's call, would have been improbable, if not impossible, apart from his ancestry. That his mind and heart were ready are a proof of his godly heritage. There would, for instance, have been no Samuel but for Hannah's prayers; no Moses but for Amram and Jochebed, who were not afraid of the king's commandment; and no Apostle Paul had he not been able to say: "I thank God Whom I serve from my forefathers."

All this Hudson Taylor himself acknowledged when he wrote: "For myself, and the work I have been permitted to do for God, I owe an unspeakable debt of gratitude to my beloved and honoured parents who have entered into rest, but the influence of whose lives will never pass away."

It is to this ancestry we must now refer.

III

A GODLY HERITAGE

"O BEAUTIFUL HEREDITY," wrote the late Bishop Handley Moule, "where the Lord has so blessed the influence of the elder life that its very type is repeated in the younger, so that in a certain sense the son has not faith only but the parents' faith." This was so with Hudson Taylor.

Spiritually Hudson Taylor was the child of the Methodist Revival. James and Betty Taylor, his great-grandparents, had at the time of their marriage come under the saving influence of that great movement, and ten years later they enjoyed the honour of receiving John Wesley himself under the roof of their cottage in Barnsley. It was in this home, at the top of Old Mill Lane, the first Methodist Class Meeting in Barnsley was formed, and the first Methodist "Church in the House" gathered together for worship.

Those were rough and rude days in England's history, and Barnsley, "famous for all manner of wickedness," to quote *John Wesley's Journal,* was a stem and Spartan school for any uncompromising follower of Jesus Christ. But James Taylor never shrank from openly and publicly testifying to his Lord and Master, though he often had more than scorn and jeers to face. He well knew what it was to be stoned and roughly handled, to be dragged in the dirt, even to be in danger of his life, and on one occasion to have powdered glass rubbed in his eyes; and all for the Master's sake.

But in all these things he, with Betty his wife, learned to turn the other cheek to his tormentors. The storms without only made home more dear, and in Betty, James Taylor found a worthy partner, and a loving helpmeet in every affliction. She also became a Class leader among the Methodists, and that humble cottage home became a recognised centre of blessing and a place where God's Name was honoured. Though their worldly goods were few they knew how to be rich towards God, and rejoiced to lay aside each week, as God's portion, one-tenth, and even more, of their scanty income of thirteen shillings and sixpence a week. In these and other ways they bequeathed to their children, and to their children's children, that richest of all inheritances, a godly tradition and example.

But the wedded life of this worthy couple was comparatively short, for when their eldest son was but a youth of seventeen the father died leaving a widow and several children. But before his death one of his great ambitions had been achieved. He had seen, and had a part in, the building and opening of the first Wesleyan Chapel in Barnsley.

Happily John, the eldest son, though still young, had learned the trade of a linen-reed maker, and was able to shoulder no small share of the burden of that bereaved home. Being a hard and diligent worker John Taylor became, to quote *The Leeds Intelligencer,* "of great consequence to the stable industry of the town," so that, without neglecting his widowed mother, he at the early age of twenty-one claimed Mary Shepherd as his bride. In Mary Shepherd, a girl of Scotch extraction, and a daughter, so it is recorded, of one of John Wesley's early preachers, were added to the sturdy Yorkshire stock some of those sterling qualities associated with the North of the Tweed.

John and Mary Taylor, in their new home, took up the torch of truth James Taylor had bequeathed, and were prospered in their business, as well as in the things of God. A new home was built on Pitt Street, not far from the Wesleyan Manse, and their children, who became familiar with the Wesleyan Minister's family, were allowed to choose, within certain limits, their own line in life. One joined his father in business, one became a stockbroker in Manchester, one became a Wesleyan minister, and James, the father of Hudson Taylor, though ambitious to become a doctor, had to be satisfied with the less expensive training of a chemist. To this end he was early apprenticed to a friend in the neighbouring town of Rotherham.

This James Taylor, named after his grandfather of Old Mill Lane, was a sturdy youth, short and active, with a well-knit figure. He grew up to be a powerful and forceful man. He was an omnivorous reader, a painstaking student, a mathematician of no mean order, and one possessed of a capacity for thoroughness and determination well calculated to make him master of anything he took in hand. At the age of nineteen he was welcomed as an accredited local preacher on to the plan of the Wesleyan Methodist Church, and he soon became, by reason of his thoughtful and well-prepared sermons, combined with unusual powers of speech, a popular and acceptable preacher. While still young he had, with money advanced by his father, commenced business for himself as a chemist, at 21 Cheapside, Barnsley, right in the heart of the town, and ere long seriously contemplated marriage. For seven years he had been deeply attached to Amelia Hudson, eldest daughter of Benjamin and Mrs. Hudson, the Wesleyan minister and his wife, who, according to the itinerary system of that Church, had in 1824 been appointed to Barnsley. As the home of James Taylor's childhood in Pitt Street was opposite the Wesleyan Manse, it was only natural that the young people should become acquainted one with another, and it was in this way that the attachment was formed.

The Hudsons were a gifted family, the father and at least three of his children having considerable artistic talent, especially as portrait painters. One of the sons obtained some notoriety as a painter of Indian Rajahs, and was, at one time, granted sittings by Mr. W. E. Gladstone at Hawarden. Another marked gift—if it may be called such—of this family was humour in a conspicuous degree, and this saving grace was largely inherited by the Hudson Taylor of our story.

Amelia Hudson, the eldest daughter in this family, and the mother of Hudson Taylor, was educated at the Friends' School at Darlington, and went, somewhat early in life, as governess to a gentleman-farmer's family at Castle Donnington, near Derby, so that the young lovers, James Taylor and Amelia Hudson, had their fair share of the piquant experience of separation during their years of courtship. But the industry and thrift of the young chemist were rewarded, for on April 5, 1831, on the third day after his twenty-fourth birthday, with his father's loan already refunded, he married his sweet bride, who was just a year younger than himself. Their home was established in Cheapside, right in the heart of Barnsley.

Five children came to gladden their parents' hearts; James Hudson, the first-born; then William Shepherd, named after his grandmother; then Amelia Hudson, subsequently the wife of Benjamin Broomhall; then Theodore, and lastly Louise Shepherd, who married William Walker, a Wesleyan minister. But though William Shepherd lived long enough to become a companion and play-fellow to his elder brother Hudson, he died quite young, while his younger brother Theodore died earlier still. It was thus but natural that a close and strong attachment should spring up between Hudson and his sister Amelia, three and a half years his junior, which bond became altogether unique and lovely, a bond which bound them almost as lovers all through their long and arduous careers.

In their parents, little Hudson and his two sisters found those who were worthy complements to one another. What the father seemed to lack the mother supplied, and *vice versa*. The father was a powerful man, at times almost too forceful for the full happiness of those he loved. His sense of duty was so strong, and his standard for life so high, that he was in danger of forgetting the limitations and frailties of human nature, especially youthful human nature. One has only to look at the portrait of his fine, strong face to see something of his strength of character and of those intellectual gifts which his brow and piercing eyes betoken. His gifts of speech, combined with his intense convictions and almost mesmeric influence, made him a powerful advocate. And he could hold the little company of two or three as spellbound as the larger audience. Sometimes he did use his powers of mesmerism. He hypnotised the sick to bring them sleep, and once he mesmerised a neighbour's dog which had become a public nuisance, so that it ceased henceforth its annoying bark! But though he had qualities which made men stand in awe of him, and though he was a stern disciplinarian, men learned to honour and to trust him. If he was strict with others, he was no less strict with himself. His deep sense of responsibility to God, his upright dealings with men, his scrupulous care to be honourable in all things, and his unquestioned integrity, soon commanded the esteem and confidence of his fellowmen. And behind and beneath that powerful exterior beat a large and kindly heart, for he was full of good works and gracious deeds, especially to any who were in need or sorrow.

But the mother of the home was cast in a gentler mould, yet without any touch of weakness. While always supporting the father's authority she knew how to comfort and to soothe. She, too, believed in disci pline, but her government was more by love than law. Her very presence brought a sense of calm and tranquillity, and to her quiet, loving, tactful ways young Hudson and his sisters owed no less than to their father. If he supplied the driving force of life, she poured in the oil. She was an excellent housewife, too, and with the aid of one maid made her home a model of smooth running. Slovenliness was never allowed, while dili gence, neatness, and order were unfailingly required, until they became the habits of the children.

This mother also superintended in large part the education of her children, and in this they had a good and exact teacher. If she excelled in anything it was in her knowledge of English. In this she would not suffer any slovenly use of words, any error in grammar, or defect in enunciation and pronunciation. It is not improbable that all this close attention to words and sounds, with all its consequent training of the ear, was of inestimable value to Hudson Taylor when he came to study the Chinese language, which in an especial degree demands accuracy in tone and emphasis.

But children learn more than their parents or others consciously teach them. There is an atmosphere in every home, and in every contact, which frequently makes a deeper mark than definite tuition. "Environment," said Dr. Barnardo, after long and wide experience, "is more powerful than heredity." And environment is a comprehensive term including things spiritual, intellectual and physical, as well as the general habits of life and character.

There is no question as to the spiritual influences which impressed and moulded the mind and heart of young Hudson Taylor. Before his birth his father had been deeply impressed with God's claim upon the firstborn of Israel, and he and his wife had, with God's Word in their hands, solemnly dedicated and set apart for God the child they hoped shortly to receive from the Giver of all life. And after his birth the new young life was surrounded by every influence and definite instruction that could impress him with the sense of God, and with the importance of godly living.

> SCRIPTURE TESTIMONY
>
> *Strong faith from genera-*
> *tions of prayer and example*
>
> I CORINTHIANS II:I · 2 TIMOTHY I:5

James Taylor was a man possessed of a strong, personal faith in God as the Living God, and in His unchanging faithfulness. To him nothing was more important than that his children should be imbued with the same convictions. To this end he took them with him into his closet, when he shut to the door that he might pray to his Father in secret, and in this way not only were habits of prayer taught, but a sense of the reality and presence of God was communicated to his children. Bible study was also encouraged, nay, even required, and a simple but implicit faith in the trustworthiness of God's Word was inculcated. Not only was family prayer made a sacred institution, but a definite time was set apart in each day's programme for the young people's private devotions.

All this early training in childlike faith in God, and in God's promises, was of inestimable value to Hudson Taylor in years to come. Foundations were then laid in things of the Spirit without which many of the constructive enterprises of the future would have been impossible.

And James Taylor, the father, was as downright and thorough in the details of his business as in the realm of the soul. Indeed, he would not separate the two, for he carried his sense of God into everything. Utter rectitude in all financial undertakings, no matter how small, was part of his religion. To keep a man waiting one day for the payment of a debt was in his view to rob the man of money. And although he was a chemist, his gifts in matters of finance, his scrupulous regard for detail, and his exactitude in the realm of mathematics, led his townsmen to appoint him as Manager to the Barnsley Permanent Building Society.[1] The man who

---

1   James Taylor was one of the founders of the Barnsley Permanent Building Society, and manager from 1853 to 1875. He retired from his original business, as chemist, about 1865.

had been accustomed to weigh out his prescriptions to a gram, or a grain, set himself to compile tables of interest, at different rates, to four and five places of decimals, and to prepare his own tables of logarithms to assist in his calculations. Small wonder was it that the double duties of chemist and manager became too heavy, so that he ultimately sold his business, and devoted himself to the work of the Building Society. But this was after young Hudson had left the home, but not before this precision and ability in money and other matters had been inherited and acquired by the son. And in all this one recognises God's chosen school for Hudson Taylor, in view of his future responsibilities.

It is easy to see how Hudson Taylor was enriched by the joint contribution of both his parents. From them he inherited that strength of character, that resolute determination to do his duty, that unshaken faith in God, which carried him through many a seemingly impossible task; that love and consideration for others, and that gentle humble spirit which in honour preferred others to himself. What made him so approachable were those gentle qualities inherited from his mother; yet beneath all these, though not always seen by men, were those powerful reserves of strength and resolution, and that almost lion-like determination, bequeathed him by his father.

IV

A MAN SENT FROM GOD

JAMES HUDSON Taylor was born at Barnsley on the 21st of May 1832. As we have seen there was nothing nebulous in the home into which he came as first-born. Strong, godly influences surrounded him from the beginning. Heaven lay about him in his infancy. He saw it in his mother's face, and it was evident in his father's faith. He was taught, as a child, to believe in God, and to see God in His handiwork.

Young Hudson was a delicate lad, and was for long unable to go to school. Save for a period of about two years, up to the Christmas of 1845, when he was nearly fourteen years of age, all his tuition was received at home. There was definite loss, and yet real gain, in this arrangement. While he missed that discipline which a public school affords, he profited by the stimulating energies of his father and the gentle and exact teaching of his mother. Most of his studies were directed by his mother, but his father, himself a man of great mental energy—he commenced the study of Chinese, for instance, when nearly seventy years of age—took the personal oversight of certain subjects, so that before young Hudson was more than four years of age he had learned the Hebrew alphabet on his father's knee. That his natural abilities were good his whole life proved, and many a young missionary has been amazed and disconcerted to hear him say that an elementary working knowledge of Chinese could be acquired in six months!

And it was by the early conversations of his father— and what a powerful conversationalist his father was— that young Hudson, when only four or five years of age, became deeply impressed with the need of the heathen world. At this youthful period he was often heard to say: "When I am a man I will be a missionary, and go to China."

James Taylor, who had read several books on China, and especially *The Travels of Captain Basil Hall,* had for long been deeply moved by the spiritual need of that country. As his own way to definite missionary work was closed, he frequently prayed that, if God gave him a son, that son might devote his life to that vast and needy land. Yet he never told his son of these prayers until seven years after he had actually sailed for China. But the information imparted, and the prayers offered, were not in vain, and of James Taylor it might be said, as it was said of David: "Thou didst well in that it was in thine heart; nevertheless thou shalt not build the house; but thy son." And young Hudson early inherited his father's love of reading, and as reading aloud was encouraged and became a habit in the home, he and other inmates had their hearts and minds enlarged by many a book of travel and of history. His father, too, was a sociable man, and threw his home open to friends and visitors. This was especially the case on market days, or when the Methodist quarterly meetings were held in Barnsley. Then, in the drawing-room over the shop, many subjects were discussed, including theology, sermons, politics, and the work of God at home and abroad. And, as the young people were allowed to be present on these occasions, ineffaceable impressions were received.

Though the régime of this home was strict and Spartan, certain relaxations and lighter studies were encouraged. It was thus that Hudson began that early love of flowers, of birds, and butterflies, which continued with him through life. There was nothing he loved better than to go with his sister Amelia, or when possible with his father, into the neighbouring woods to study Nature at first-hand, and to bring specimens home. This devotion to the beautiful was a constant refreshment to him throughout his strenuous career, and his letters home from China had many a reference to the flora and fauna of that land. And it was to the care of a few chosen plants and flowers that he frequently turned for relief of mind when burdened with urgent and pressing duties.

But, to return to his youthful days in Barnsley, some of the first definite spiritual experiences in his life were connected with the Methodist Centenary celebrations in 1839, when he was only seven years old. At that time a religious revival visited parts of Yorkshire, and he used to accompany his father into the country to be present at the meetings. Though but a lad he entered heartily into the spirit of the movement, and often his young face glowed with delight when men were blessed and saved.

Methodists everywhere sought to celebrate that Centenary by undertaking new missionary adventures in various parts of the world. But nothing was planned for China, and this deeply pained James Taylor. "Why do we not send missionaries there?" he would frequently exclaim.

It is a significant fact that, in that same year, what was probably the first Protestant Missionary Atlas of the World was published in London. And in that atlas there was no map of China! The sad fact was that there was no need for a map of China in a missionary Atlas of the World in 1839, for the one and only missionary centre, where Robert Morrison had laboured for twenty- seven years, could be and was marked upon the map of Asia. But Morrison had been dead five years, and practically nothing more had been attempted since by any British Missionary Society, for China was then deemed a closed land.

It was about this time that Hudson Taylor and his sister Amelia became deeply interested in a book known as *Peter Parley's China*. This book they read again and again, until the sister, too, resolved to accompany her brother to that strange and distant country.

When about eleven years of age young Hudson first went to school, but even then his health did not allow him to attend with any regularity. Yet it was doubtless good for him to be brought into touch with the life and discipline of school, though he knew little of the benefit of games and sport. During this brief school period he attended a camp meeting held in a park near Leeds, and there heard Mr. Henry Reed relate some of his personal experiences in Tasmania. These made a deep and lasting impression upon him, though they were unattended at that time by any definite spiritual decisions.

But these brief school-days ceased just before Christmas, 1845, when he was only thirteen years of age. Now he began to assist his father in his shop, and spent his time between the enjoyments of his father's library and the study of dispensing. In 1846, when fourteen years of age, he made his first definite surrender of himself to God. This was brought about through the reading of a leaflet published by the Religious Tract Society, and concerning this experience he wrote some few years later :

> "From my earliest childhood I have felt the strivings of the Holy Spirit, and when about fourteen years of age I gave my heart to God."

In the following year he obtained a post in a Barnsley bank, but in consequence of serious eye trouble, caused by much writing by gas-light, this position was relinquished after being held for only nine months. None the less, this brief banking experience proved highly useful in his future career.

But the worldly associates, and especially the influence of one man in the bank, made him for a time set his heart on wealth and worldly pleasures, and predisposed him towards their sceptical and infidel teaching. Strange as it may seem, in after life he wrote, "I have often been thankful for this time of scepticism," and the reason for this is best given in his own words:

> "The inconsistencies of Christian people, who, while professing to believe their Bibles, were yet content to live just as they would if there were no such Book, had been one of the strongest arguments of my sceptical companions; and I frequently felt at that time, and said, that if I pretended to believe the Bible I would at any rate attempt to live by it, putting it fairly to the test, and if it failed to prove true and reliable, would throw it overboard altogether. These views I retained when the Lord was pleased to bring me to Himself; and I think I may say that since then I have put God's Word to the test. Certainly it has never failed me."

But doubts are sometimes faith's shadow. With him they were the searching of his soul for solid rock upon which to place his feet, and while it is not always true that "He who never doubted never half-believed," he was unquestionably allowed to pass through those deep waters to find God's resting-place. The story of how God did bring him to Himself is best given in his own words:

"Let me tell you how God answered the prayers of my dear mother, and of my beloved sister, now Mrs. Broomhall, for my conversion. On a day which I shall never forget, when I was about fifteen[1] years of age,

SCRIPTURE TESTIMONY
Timely prayer for someone far away
MATTHEW 18:19
Gospel is the power of God for salvation
ROMANS 1:16

my dear mother being absent from home, I had a holiday, and in the afternoon looked through my father's library to find some book with which to while away the unoccupied hours. Nothing attracting me, I turned over a little basket of pamphlets, and selected from amongst them a Gospel tract which looked interesting, saying to myself, 'there will be a story at the commencement, and a sermon or moral at the close: I will take the former and leave the latter for those who like it.'

"I sat down to read the little book in an utterly unconcerned state of mind, believing indeed at the time that if there were any salvation it was not for me, and with a distinct intention to put away the tract as soon as it should seem prosy. I may say that it was not uncommon in those days to call conversion 'becoming serious,' and judging by the faces of some of its professors, it appeared to be a very serious matter indeed. Would it not be well if the people of God had always tell-tale faces, evincing the blessings and gladness of salvation so clearly that unconverted people might have to call conversion 'becoming joyful' instead of 'becoming serious'?

---

1 This should read "seventeen years of age," see footnote on p. 7. It was the summer of 1849.

"Little did I know at the time what was going on in the heart of my dear mother, seventy or eighty miles away. She rose from the dinner-table that afternoon with an intense yearning for the conversion of her boy, and feeling that— absent from home, and having more leisure than she could otherwise secure—a special opportunity was afforded her of pleading with God on my behalf. She went to her room and turned the key in the door, resolved not to leave that spot until her prayers were answered. Hour after hour did that dear mother plead for me, until at length she could pray no longer, but was constrained to praise God for that which His Spirit taught her had already been accomplished—the conversion of her only son.

"I in the meantime had been led in the way I have mentioned to take up this little tract, and while reading it was struck with the sentence, 'the finished work of Christ.' The thought passed through my mind, 'Why does the author use this expression? why not say the atoning or propitiatory work of Christ?' Immediately the words 'It is finished' suggested themselves to my mind. What was finished? And I at once replied, 'A full and perfect atonement and satisfaction for sin: the debt was paid by the Substitute; Christ died for our sins, and not for ours only, but also for the sins of the whole world.' Then came the thought, 'If the whole work was finished and the whole debt paid, what is there left for me to do'? And with this dawned the joyful conviction, as light was flashed into my soul by the Holy Spirit, that there was nothing in the world to be done but to fall down on one's knees, and accepting this Saviour and His salvation, to praise Him for evermore. Thus while my dear mother was praising God on her knees in her chamber, I was praising Him in the old warehouse to which I had gone alone to read at my leisure this little book.

"Several days elapsed ere I ventured to make my beloved sister the confidante of my joy, and then only after she had promised not to tell anyone of my soul secret. When our dear mother came home a fortnight later, I was the first to meet her at the door, and to tell her I had such glad news to give. I can almost feel that dear mother's arms around my neck, as she pressed me to her bosom and said, 'I know, my boy; I have been rejoicing for a fortnight in the glad tidings you have to tell me.' 'Why,' I asked in surprise, 'has Amelia broken her promise? She said she would tell no one.' My dear mother assured me that it was not from any human source that she had learned the tidings, and went on to tell the little incident mentioned above. You will agree with me that it would be strange indeed if I were not a believer in the power of prayer.

"Nor was this all. Some little time after, I picked up a pocket-book exactly like one of my own, and thinking that it was mine, opened it. The lines that caught my eye were an entry in the little diary, which belonged to my sister, to the effect that she would give herself daily to prayer until God should answer in the conversion of her brother. Exactly one month later the Lord was pleased to turn me from darkness to light."

It was not many months after the experiences recorded above that, having a leisure afternoon, he repaired to his own room to spend it alone with God. It was then that he experienced that overwhelming sense of God, and of God's claim upon him, which has been already recorded in the earlier pages of this book. But his path was not uncheckered. Between that June afternoon in his father's library and the Sunday in early December when the insistent call to China came, young Hudson Taylor knew something of that spiritual struggle of which the Apostle wrote so vividly when he said: "I delight in the law of God after the inward man; but I see a different law in my members, warring against the law of my mind and bringing me into captivity under the law of sin."

Yet, on the one hand, he and his sister Amelia had begun definite work for God in some of the poorer parts of the town. But, on the other hand, he had to confess that "the first joys of conversion passed away after a time, and were succeeded by a period of painful deadness of soul, with much conflict." This condition of conflict lasted through the autumn. What still remains of his own writings at that time reveal his joy and his participation in a work of grace at Pitt Street Chapel, when about one hundred decisions for Christ were re-corded, and yet, on the other hand, they show his feeling, to quote his own words, that "something was wrong, so wrong that I feared I might fall away from grace and be finally lost."

The crisis came on Sunday, December 2, 1849, when he was seventeen years of age. Being kept at home with a cold he wrote to his sister Amelia, who was then at school in Barton-on-Humber:

> "Pray for me, dear Amelia, pray for me. I am seeking entire sanctification. Oh that the Lord would take away my heart of stone and give me a heart of flesh! Mr. Simmons gave us our tickets last Sunday. The verse is: 'then will I sprinkle clean water upon you, and ye shall be clean.' (Ezekiel 36:25, etc.). Oh that I could take hold of the blessed promises of God's Holy Word! My heart longs for perfect holiness."

And this prayer was answered sooner than he had expected, for on that very day the Lord whom he sought came suddenly to His temple, and a covenant was sealed between Hudson Taylor and his God. It was then when he besought God to restore him to full communion, and promised, to quote his own words, "If God would only save me completely, then I would do anything in his cause He might direct," that God took him at his word and visited him with His salvation.

> "Never shall I forget," to quote again his words already recorded, "the feeling that came over me then. Words can never describe it. I felt I was in the presence of God, entering into covenant with the Almighty. I felt as though I wished to withdraw my promise but could not. Something seemed to say 'Your prayer is answered, your conditions are accepted,' and from that time the conviction never left me that I was called to China."

Though the day was far spent it was not too late to let his sister know that the prayer for which he had asked had been already answered and so the envelope was opened, and a brief postscript added to the letter quoted above, and this added note reveals the abundant joy which had now become his.

"Bless the Lord, O my soul, and all that is within me shout His praise! Glory to God, my dear Amelia. Christ has said: 'seek, and ye shall find,' and praise His Name, He has revealed Himself to me in an overflowing manner. He has cleansed me from all sin, from all my idols. He has given me a new heart. Glory, glory, glory, to His ever-blessed Name! I cannot write for joy. I open my letter to tell you."

V

GOD AND GOD ONLY

HUDSON TAYLOR was not disobedient to the heavenly vision. Though his emotional nature had been deeply moved it took with him an eminently practical turn. He immediately sought to make himself acquainted with, and ready for, the unknown land of China. A Mr. Whitworth, the local Treasurer of the British and Foreign Bible Society, obtained for him a copy of *St. Luke's Gospel* in the Mandarin dialect, and another friend, the Congregational minister, lent him a copy of Medhurst's *China*.

The spirit in which these books were sought is best told by himself. Having explained to the Congregational minister the reason for borrowing Medhurst's *China*,

SCRIPTURE TESTIMONY
Childlike faith required to enter Kingdom of God
MATTHEW 18:3 · LUKE 18:17

namely, that God had called him to missionary service in that land, his friend inquired:

> "And how do you propose to go there? "
> "I answered," wrote Hudson Taylor, "that I did not at all know; that it seemed to be probable that I should need to do as the Twelve and Seventy had done in Judea, go without purse or scrip, relying on Him who had sent me to supply all my need."

29

"Kindly placing his hand on my shoulder the minister replied, 'Ah, my boy, as you grow older you will become wiser than that. Such an idea would do very well in the days when Christ Himself was on earth, but not now.'"

Many years later, when commenting on this episode, Hudson Taylor added:

"I have grown older since then, but not wiser. I am more and more convinced that if we were to take the directions of our Master, and the assurance He gave to His first disciples, more fully as our guide, we should find them just as suited to our times as to those in which they were originally given."

And this childlike confidence and simplicity were throughout the dominant characteristics of his life.

Medhurst's *China* was devoured, and *St. Luke's Gospel* in Chinese was so carefully and diligently studied, by the comparison of verses in which the same words occurred, that, though he possessed no dictionary, he mastered in a few weeks over five hundred Chinese characters.

> **SCRIPTURE TESTIMONY**
>
> *Walk by the Spirit to discipline the flesh*
>
> I CORINTHIANS 9:24-27 ·
> I CORINTHIANS 10:23 · GALATIANS 5:16

With this zeal in study he combined self-discipline and self-denial as other means of preparation. His feather-bed, so commonly used in Yorkshire, was dispensed with; open-air exercise was made a duty, and personal work among the sick and poor was eagerly sought. Through Mr. Whitworth also he became acquainted with two magazines, *The Watchman* and *The Gleaner*, and through these he was brought into touch with various agencies at work for God in the world, and among these especially with the newly formed organization, "The Chinese Association," afterwards known as "The Chinese Evangelization Society."

This Association, undenominational in character, aimed at employing Chinese evangelists throughout China, and was closely associated with Dr. Gutzlaff, a man of many gifts and apostolic fervour, but whose zeal sometimes outran his discretion. But Gutzlaff's passion for the evangelization of

China produced an extraordinary enthusiasm in Europe and England, some of his journeys on the Continent being almost of a triumphal character.

Hudson Taylor, being brought into touch with this work, set himself to further it in every possible way, and thus commenced a correspondence with Mr. George Pearse, the Secretary of the Chinese Evangelization Society, under which he eventually went out to China.

Though Gutzlaff's work was rather discredited, and though he died of a broken heart when he learned how he had been deceived by his Chinese agents, his labours were not in vain, and Hudson Taylor in later life sometimes spoke of him as the grandfather of the China Inland Mission.

All this time Hudson Taylor had continued in his father's business, studying Latin, Greek, Theology and Medicine, and losing no opportunity to qualify himself for his life's work. And deep exercise of heart was part of this preparation. In many ways his devotion was tested and tried, and increasingly he found himself shut up unto God. With him it was to be God and God alone.

Among the sifting experiences of this testing time was a youthful attachment to one of his sister's friends, for, after many months of ardent love, time showed him that to win and claim her he must sacrifice China. Yet poignant as this trial was he remained loyal to God's call. But how was he to go?

> "The Wesleyans have no stations in China," he wrote, "the established Church have one or two, but I am not a Churchman... the Baptists and the Independents have stations there, but I do not hold their views. The Chinese Association is very low in funds."

To some these things might have become valid arguments in favour of remaining at home, and especially so when love beckoned. But it was not so with him. "So God and God alone is my hope," he added, "and I need no other."

Steadily but surely he was being shut up to God Himself, to find in Him, and Him alone, his all-sufficient supply.

But finding that he could not make good progress with Chinese without a dictionary, he resolved to concentrate upon the study of medicine. He had been with his father for five years, apart from the nine months at the bank, and he now began to seek employment in a surgery, where he might acquire medical and surgical skill. In this his prayers were answered, for one of his aunts, on his mother's side, was married to the brother of Dr. Robert Hardey of Hull, where an opening was obtained for him.

Dr. Hardey not only had a large general practice, but had also the surgical oversight of some factories, in addition to being lecturer in the local School of Medicine. Here young Hudson Taylor, on May 21, 1851, his nineteenth birthday, took up his new duties. For the next sixteen months Hull was his home, and here he passed through stern spiritual discipline and training, all of which were to strip him of self-confidence, and demand a larger and an utter devotion of himself to God.

Residing at first with the doctor he subsequently moved to live with his aunt, the cost of his board being provided by the doctor. But as he felt he must tithe this new supply, as he did all his other earnings, he found it necessary to seek less expensive lodgings. This led him to a humble cottage at Drainside, where he rented a bedsitting room for three shillings a week. Brought thus into close contact with poverty and suffering, he soon began to give away, not merely one-tenth of his income, but actually two-thirds, by the practice of many rigid economies. It was a school of simple and stem living, accompanied by many and varied blessings.

Writing to his mother, whose love treasured up every trifle that concerned her boy, he discloses the following illuminating particulars of his daily fare. And the recital reveals the man, so precise, and accurate, and careful in matters of detail, that part of this letter deserves to be quoted. If any man was faithful in that which was least it was Hudson Taylor.

> "I have found some brown biscuits which are really as cheap as bread, eighteen pence a stone, and much nicer. For breakfast I have biscuit and herring, which is cheaper than butter (three for a penny and half a one is enough) with coffee. For dinner I have at present a prune-and-apple pie. Prunes are two or three pence a pound and apples tenpence a peck. I use no sugar but loaf, which I powder, and at four- pence halfpenny a pound I find it is cheaper than the coarser kind. Sometimes I have roast

potatoes and tongue, which is as inexpensive as any other meat. For tea I have biscuit and apples. I take no supper, or occasionally a little biscuit and apple. Sometimes I have a rice pudding, a few peas boiled instead of potatoes, and now and then some fish. By being wide awake, I can get cheese at fourpence to sixpence a pound that is better than we often have at home for eight- pence. Now I see rhubarb and lettuce in the market, so I shall soon have another change. I pickled a penny red cabbage with three halfpence worth of vinegar, which made me a large jar-full. So you see, at little expense I enjoy many comforts. To these add a home where every want is anticipated, and 'the peace of God which passeth all understanding,' and if I were not happy and contented I should deserve to be miserable."

But the passion of his soul breaks away from these material things, and he reveals the unquenchable fire burning in his heart, when he writes:

"Continue to pray for me, dear Mother. Though comfortable as regards temporal matters, and happy and thankful, I feel I need your prayers.... Oh, Mother, I cannot tell you, I cannot describe how I long to be a missionary; to carry the Glad Tidings to poor, perishing sinners; to spend and be spent for Him who died for me. I feel as if for this I could give up everything, every idol, however dear."

Of the varied experiences through which he passed in those days in Hull we can but dwell on two. There was first the deep soul struggle connected with his attachment to Miss V., to which reference has already been made. Much as this struggle of two years cost him, for the attachment was deep and real, he remained true to his call. That was to be supreme, and alone he faced the issue and overcame, though his sister was his loved confidante throughout this supreme test.

"Thank God," he wrote to her when finally the matter was settled, "the way of duty is the safe way."

The other great question was, Could he so trust God, and so move God by prayer, while in the homeland, as to justify him in venturing forth to a dark and distant country? In many ways this vital question was put to the test.

"When I get out to China," he said to himself, "I shall have no claim on anyone for anything. My only claim will be on God. How important to learn before leaving England, to move man through God by prayer alone.... I had not at that time learned that even 'if we believe not, yet He abideth faithful, He cannot deny Himself.' It was consequently a very serious question to my mind, not whether He was faithful, but whether I had strong enough faith to warrant my embarking in the enterprise set before me."

SCRIPTURE TESTIMONY

Give to everyone who asks

MATTHEW 5:42 · LUKE 6:30 · ACTS 20:35 · 2 CORINTHIANS 8:1-2 · I JOHN 3:17

Two lessons in this school of faith were now learned which were a help to him for the rest of his life, and to these reference must be made. Though his employer had requested him to remind him when his salary was due, he determined not to do this, that he might thus test his faith. On one occasion his quarterly salary was due but no allusion had been made to it, and he found himself with only two shillings and sixpence in his pocket. At this juncture he was asked by a poor man to go and pray with his wife who was dying. He went and found a squalid room in which were four or five half-starved children, and their mother, lying on a wretched pallet, with a three-day-old babe crying at her breast. The clamant need of this poor woman, and his own limited circumstances, led to a spiritual conflict such as he said he had never experienced before, and possibly never since. He tried to pray but could not. He felt it would be mocking God to ask His aid while he withheld his own half-crown, and yet—that was all he had! Had it been two shillings and a sixpence he could have given part, but it was a half-crown piece, so his gift must be all or nothing. In vain he tried to speak words of comfort, until he felt a hypocrite himself, since he could not trust God with an empty pocket. Filled with distress he rose at length from his knees, only to have the distracted father say to him, "If you can help us, for God's sake do." At that moment the Lord's words, "Give to him that asketh of thee," flashed through his mind, and, as he said afterwards, "In the word of a King there is power." Thrusting his hand into his pocket he drew out his last and only coin, and gave it to the man. The struggle had been keen and crucial, but joy now flooded his soul.

> "Not only was the poor woman's life saved," he subsequently wrote, "but my life, as I fully realised, had been saved too. It might have been a wreck—probably would have been as a Christian life—had not grace at that time conquered and the striving of God's Spirit been obeyed."

Home he went that night with a heart as light as his pocket, but with the dark, deserted streets resounding with his praise. Before retiring to rest he asked the Lord that the loan might be a short one, for otherwise he would have no dinner next day. The morning came and with it the postman, who delivered a letter containing half a sovereign and a pair of gloves! "Four hundred per cent for twelve hours' investment!" he exclaimed, and there and then determined that God's bank, that could not break, should henceforth have his savings or his earnings, as the case might be.

But the test did not cease here. This ten shillings, though made to last a fortnight, came all too soon to its end, and yet the doctor had not alluded to his salary. It was now not a case of salary with him but rather of "Can I go to China?" He had only to ask the doctor and the money would be his, but then the proof of the power of prayer to move men would be lost, and that to him was more than the cash. Saturday afternoon came, when unexpectedly the doctor said, "By the way, Taylor, is not your salary due?" With deep emotion Hudson Taylor replied that it was, only to be greeted with the words, "I am so sorry you did not remind me... for only this afternoon I sent all the money I had to the bank." His sudden elation immediately gave way to deepest disappointment. Not only did he need money himself for food, but his rent was due, and his landlady was a poor woman. Yet prayer brought calm and confidence that God would work in some yet unknown way.

But the hours sped by, and though he lingered longer than usual the time came when he could do no other than turn down the gas and go. At that moment who should enter the surgery but the doctor, laughing heartily and asking for the ledger. Odd as it seemed, a wealthy patient, at that late hour had called to pay his bill. Though he could have sent a cheque at any time, he had felt constrained to come at that unusual time to discharge his liability. And so, unlikely as it had appeared, Hudson Taylor received his salary, and went home with a joyful heart!

> "Again I was left," he wrote, "my feelings undiscovered, to go back to my little closet and praise the Lord with a joyful heart that after all *I might go to China.* To me," he added, "this incident was not a trivial one; and to recall it, sometimes in circumstances of great difficulty in China or elsewhere, has proved no small comfort and strength."

Yet another serious test arose during those days at Hull. China filled his heart, and he was ready for anything that would bless that land. He had even written to his mother to say that, if his father would go to China, he would willingly stay at home to manage the business and work like a slave to support him.

> "Tell him," he wrote, "the voyage would probably lengthen his life. He has a gift for languages.... Does he not think there are plenty of Christians in Barnsley? But who cares for China? They are dying, dying, dying, two hundred and fifty thousand every week without the knowledge of God, of Christ, of salvation. Oh, let us look with compassion on this multitude!"

But an entirely different and crushing proposition came from his father. It was that Hudson Taylor should come home and manage the business while he, the father, went to Canada, or the United States, where he thought a larger and more useful sphere than Barnsley might be found. The conflict that followed between filial piety and China's call was a battle royal. He felt he could not agree, and said so. But here again he felt he must overcome by prayer and not by self-will, and so he wrote a deeply penitent letter to his father in which the following words occur:

"If you still wish me to come home for two years I will do so willingly, nay with pleasure, as it will give me an opportunity of showing the sincerity of my repentance. Then afterwards, if the Lord will, I shall hope to engage in His work in China."

In this letter he was offering up his Isaac, his God- given ambition, and it was accepted but not required. The opportunity was given back to him, as by a resurrection from the dead, to be more sacred than ever.

But his residence at Hull was not characterised by trial only, for it was during those months that he was enriched by many a helpful fellowship and influence. By a combination of circumstances he was brought into touch with the Plymouth Brethren and other undenominational movements, which prepared him for his future interdenominational activities. Shortly before leaving Barnsley he had joined the Wesleyan Reformers when they separated themselves from the parent body in 1849, since, to quote his own words, he had not been "able to reconcile the late proceedings with the doctrines and precepts of Holy Scripture." This had made him more ready to study Church history and Church government, and prepared him for fellowship with other believers, and at Hull he found great spiritual help from the ministry of Mr. Andrew Jukes, who, though previously in Anglican Orders, had become a distinguished teacher among the Brethren. And through the Hull meeting he was brought into touch with George Müller of Bristol, and with other work of a similar nature.

At this time he also learned of the visit of the German missionary Lobscheid to London, and in his zeal to learn all he could about China he and his sister Amelia paid what was to them a memorable visit to the great metropolis.

But his interview with Mr. Lobscheid was not exactly encouraging, for that good man warned him that with his light-coloured hair and grey-blue eyes he would be more than ever called, "the red-haired devil." But Hudson Taylor was not daunted by such things as this, indeed he never was daunted if conscious of God's call.

But what made the London visit most worth while was his interview with Mr. George Pearse, the Secretary of the Chinese Evangelization Society, and his introduction to that circle of friends—some of the excellent of all the earth—at Bruce Grove, Tottenham. Then commenced an intimate and life-long friendship with the family of the Howards, and others, who had been interested in China already. One of this distinguished family had been in correspondence with Robert Morrison, and two of them, since Gutzlaff's visit, had been members of the Committee of the Chinese Evangelization Society. It was in this way that Hudson Taylor found some who were to be his staunch and generous helpers for life. Slowly, but surely, he was being brought into touch with new circles and new connections, all of which were part of God's plan for the future.

And now London became the next step on his way to China. In this city he thought he could make better progress with his medical studies, but how to proceed was not clear. Faith was tested, yet strengthened at every step. If his father had offered assistance in case of need he would have resigned his position in Hull immediately, but ought he to go to London without a situation, simply trusting God? After much inward debating he decided to take no anxious thought as to what he should eat or drink, but trust in God alone. The inward call was as fire in his bones.

> "I feel as if I could not live if something is not done for China," he wrote to his Mother.

So in August, 1852, he gave Dr. Hardey notice.

> "My mind is quite as much at rest," he wrote, "nay, more than it would be if I had a hundred pounds in my pocket. May He keep me ever thus."

Here we see, in the youth of twenty, the spirit of the man who was being fitted for larger trusts in days to come.

It was not long after this that an uncle in London offered him a home if he could find employment, while the Chinese Evangelization Society offered to pay his hospital fees. In September he wrote to his sister:

> "Now I have a home to go to, money to pay the fees at the Ophthalmic Hospital as well as the course at the London.... When He sees fit, *if* He sees fit, He will find me a suitable situation, and if not, He will provide for and occupy me as seems best to

Him.... Last Autumn I was fretting and stewing, reckoning and puzzling about how to manage this and that... but it all came to nothing. Now when the Lord opens the way, though everything seems adverse, He first removes one difficulty and then another, plainly saying, 'Be still and know that I am God.'.. I will not trust in my bow nor shall my sword save me. 'In God we boast all the day long.'"

VI

A GOD WHO RAISETH THE DEAD

I T WAS already dark when Hudson Taylor reached London on Saturday evening, September 25, 1852. As the small coasting vessel, which had come from Hull, encountered fog in the river it was obliged to cast anchor in the Thames and await daylight. This circumstance gave Hudson Taylor a quiet week-end for waiting upon God, and this he much needed, as his outlook was, humanly speaking, as obscure as the dark and foggy river. But none the less he was, as he wrote to his mother, "in good health and perfect peace because trusting in God."

Upon one point he had been uncertain. His father had promised to bear all his expenses in London, while, at the same time, the Chinese Evangelization Society offered to do the same. The question was which offer should he accept, or should he decline them both and seek to prove God as his one and all-sufficient confidence. After mature deliberation he determined upon the latter course. No one but God would know, for his father would conclude that the Society was assisting him, while the Society would believe that the father was behind his boy. And so, in the mighty metropolis of London, Hudson Taylor sought more fully to prove the God who had been his Helper in Hull.

Sharing an attic with a cousin in a house near Soho Square, where his uncle, Benjamin Hodson, boarded, he soon found himself in a new and worldly atmosphere. The light and frivolous distractions of London, after his quiet life in the North, grieved and tried his spirit; and when he found the Honorary Secretary of the Chinese Evangelization Society too busy to see him, and learned from his clerk of the various formalities which must precede even an interview with the Committee, his eager and expectant spirit received a rather rude shock.

Had he possessed a substantial balance in the bank it would have been comparatively easy to wait, but with only a very light purse in his pocket it was another matter. Though prepared to exercise the utmost frugality, it was a serious thing with him to contemplate detention in that busy city with nothing decisive arranged. But though his faith was tried he was not wanting in manly independence. Since he feared the Society was in danger of too much red tape and unnecessary formalities, he was quite prepared to stand alone with God, and wrote to his mother: "Thank God, I am quite as willing to lose as to gain by their assistance."

It was at this trying juncture that he received from his father an offer of a partnership in the business at Barnsley if he would come home. But, though suspense is one of life's keenest tests, he wavered not through unbelief. He was learning to walk alone with God, and enjoyed God's blessing in so doing.

His cousin, whose attic he shared, had at first been scornful of Hudson Taylor's faith, and did not fail to suggest that these delays proved that faith was fruitless. But when Tom Hodson saw his cousin's faith unshaken by adversity, he was deeply impressed, and ere long yielded himself to God's almighty love. With such encouragement Hudson Taylor felt he could afford to stand and bide God's time.

And after a month's delay the way opened for him to commence his medical studies at the London Hospital. As he still continued to share his cousin's attic near Soho Square, this entailed an eight-mile walk each day, to and from the Hospital, for his resources were far too meagre to afford sixpence a day in bus fares. In fact, he was only spending threepence a day on food, which consisted almost exclusively of brown bread and water, with a few cheap apples for lunch! A twopenny loaf, cut in two, sufficed for supper and breakfast; and, lest he should be tempted to indulge in more than a half for his evening meal, he asked the baker to divide the loaf for him. This was frugal fare indeed for a medical student walking eight miles a day; but he was proving thus his zeal in the things of God, as others have shown their zeal in the realms of art and science.

Still faith did not always come easily, and his dogged determination was at times severely taxed.

"Though the heavens have seemed as brass," he wrote, "and I have felt myself left and forsaken, I have been enabled to cling to the promises by simple naked faith, as father calls it."

Such words as these were not lightly written, as one or two episodes in his life in London prove.

The husband of his former landlady in Hull was Chief Officer in a ship which sailed from London, and Hudson Taylor, ever willing to assist, offered to receive this man's monthly half-pay and remit the same to Hull to save the woman a commission. On one occasion, as he was working for a scholarship, and could not very well spare time to call at the office, he advanced the money out of his own pocket. But when he did call he was informed, much to his consternation, that as the officer had deserted, and gone off to the gold diggings, his pay had been stopped. Hudson Taylor knew it was useless to ask the woman in Hull to refund what he had advanced, and, somewhat philosophically, recognized that, at the most, it meant that the day when he would have been cast upon God for fresh supplies was only being forestalled.

But this was not all, for soon after this he poisoned his finger when dissecting the body of a person who had died from a malignant fever. Sudden and severe sickness ensued, and the demonstrator, a skilful surgeon at the hospital, urged him to drive home in a hansom at full speed, for, said he, "you are a dead man."

But to take a hansom was not possible without the means to pay; yet even then the thought which most distressed him was, "Is China an empty dream after all?" But an assurance that he would live, and not die before his work was done, took possession of him, and though exceedingly ill he set out to walk the four miles home. But his strength failed him, and only after much suffering did he succeed in reaching his room by the aid of a bus.

The weeks which followed were full of pain, and for a time his life literally hung in the balance. At length, however, after a prolonged period of acute prostration, he was able to leave his room. Now he was urged by the doctor to go home, into the country, for much-needed refreshment. But he had no money for his fare, and he had withheld even the news of his illness from his parents. What then was he to do?

At this juncture it was deeply impressed upon him that he should call again at the Shipping Offices and make fresh inquiries. This seemed a hopeless undertaking. The office was two miles away; he had no money even for a bus, and he was so weak he had even to seek assistance in going downstairs. After all, what was the use of going? Was not this an empty impulse, he asked himself, the mere clutching at a straw, or some mental process of his own, as a last resort, and not God's guidance? But no, he felt the impulse was God-given, and so he set out, to quote his own words, "Not to *attempt* to walk, but to *walk* to Cheapside."

This incident reveals not only the strength of Hudson Taylor's convictions and his dogged determination, but, what is more, his own sense of humour. This comes out in his account of this grim walk.

> "Although undoubtedly strengthened by faith," he wrote, "I never took so much interest in shop windows as I did upon that journey I At every second or third step, I was glad to lean a little against the plate glass, and take time to examine the contents of the windows before passing on!"

It was a long two miles to the city, especially as there was then no Holborn Viaduct to save the dip down into, and the slow climb up from, Farringdon Street; and when at length he did reach his destination he was obliged to rest outside on the doorstep, despite the curious gaze of City men, ere he mounted the stairs to the office. But faith and endurance were rewarded. The money previously withheld, and more since due, was actually waiting for him, for it had been discovered that the man who had deserted was not the officer in question, but an able-bodied seaman of the same name. And thus he obtained not only what was sufficient for his journey home, but the balance for remitting to the officer's wife in Hull.

The mere recital of these experiences to the doctor who had attended him, who was a sceptic, called forth the following remark, uttered with tears in his eyes, "I would give all the world for a faith like yours." And who can say how timely that testimony was, for these two never met again. A sudden stroke, followed by a brief period of helpless waiting in the country, and the doctor's last call came. "I cannot but entertain the hope," wrote Hudson Taylor, "that the Master was speaking to him through His dealings with me, and that I shall meet him in the Better Land."

Meanwhile, Hudson Taylor had gone home to Barnsley, where his joy in God's deliverance was so great that he was unable to keep the facts to himself. One result of making the secret of his past life known to his mother was that he was not allowed to live again in London on the same frugal lines, and indeed he was not equal to it.

By the end of January, 1853, he was back again in London, where he soon obtained a post as assistant to a surgeon living at St. Mary Axe, Bishopsgate. This not only brought him within easy reach of the Hospital, but it afforded him the comforts of home life after his bachelor-like experiences in Hull and London, which had extended now to some fifteen months. The friends at Tottenham also gladly welcomed him whenever he could spare the time to visit them. But unexpected developments were at hand.

In China the Taiping Rebellion had broken out and gave great promise of being a real crusade against idolatry. Its leader, Hung Siu-ts'üen, a disappointed student, but a professed convert to Christianity, having persuaded his followers that he had received special revelations from Heaven, organized them into communities which observed the Sabbath, forbade idolatry, banned opium-smoking, and offered prayers in the name of Christ. He printed and circulated a special edition of the Bible, on the cover of which he had emblazoned his newly assumed imperial arms, for he not only conceived the idea of destroying idolatry, but even aspired to the overthrow of the Manchu Dynasty.

In the spring of 1852 the Taiping rebels commenced their northward advance, and by March, 1853, had seized Nanking, an old capital of the

Empire, where they proclaimed the new dynasty under the name of *Taiping*, or "Great Peace." By this time Hung's followers numbered more than one hundred thousand men.

Immense interest was awakened by this movement in England. It was spoken of by *The Times* as "the greatest revolution the world has yet seen;" while the *North China Herald* affirmed "that the insurgents are Christians." It was no wonder that the Chinese Evangelization Society was stirred. Here appeared the great and effectual door for which they had prayed, an opportunity surpassing their highest hopes. And so it was resolved that young Hudson Taylor should be asked if he were willing to go forth without delay.

And so it came to pass, that on Saturday afternoon, June 4, 1853, Mr. Bird, one of the Secretaries of the Society, sat in his office at 17 Red Lion Square, London, writing to Hudson Taylor. But no sooner was his letter finished, and ready for posting, than a knock came at the door, and who should walk in but Hudson Taylor himself. Was this a mere coincidence? or, was it a sign of God's leading? Both parties took it as providential proof. But Hudson Taylor, none the less, resolved to await the blessing of his parents before giving his final consent. He was quite prepared to sail without going home for a last farewell; in fact he wrote:

> "I almost think it would be easiest for us not to meet than having met to part again for ever. It is easy to talk of leaving all for Christ, but when it comes to the proof—it is only as we stand complete in Him that we can go through with it. God be with you and bless you, my own dear, dear Mother, and give you to realise the preciousness of Jesus... even in the fellowship of His sufferings."

But his departure was not to be so hasty, for, having received his parents' blessing, he visited his home once more before he sailed.

PART II

1853-1865
THE YOUNG MISSIONARY
AET. 21-33

A CHOSEN VESSEL
UNTO ME
TO BEAR MY NAME
Acts 9:15

VII

FOR MY NAME'S SAKE

WITH ONLY three persons to bid him farewell, Hudson Taylor set sail for China on Monday, September 19, 1853. The vessel was the *Dumfries,* a small sailing-ship of only four hundred and seventy tons burden, and he was the solitary passenger. But the measure of this venture for Christ was not dependent upon earthly éclat.

It was a significant coincidence that on the same day the British and Foreign Bible Society passed a resolution to print immediately one million copies of the Chinese New Testament. Hudson Taylor, as he bade his mother farewell at Liverpool, was entirely ignorant of this decision; and the Society in London had possibly never so much as heard of the young man who was to be God's Apostle for the opening up of Inland China to the Gospel. But One Hand was guiding both.

It was a day never to be forgotten by mother and son, as a little book entitled *Parting Recollections,* in the mother's clear handwriting, still exists to prove. And Hudson Taylor, though he sang and prayed with unfaltering voice at the little farewell meeting in the cabin, and though he quoted to his mother those brave words of the Apostle, "None of these things move me, neither count I my life dear unto myself," was still deeply human. The anguish of his mother's heart cut him to the quick, and after they had parted he leapt ashore to embrace his mother once more and whisper

49

in her ear some words of comfort; and when words and embraces were impossible he pencilled on the blank leaf of his pocket Bible, "The Love of God which passeth knowledge. J. H. T.," and flung the little book to her on the pier.

> "Never shall I forget that day," he wrote long years afterwards. "As we passed through the dock gates, and the separation really commenced, never shall I forget the cry of anguish wrung from that mother's heart; it went through me like a knife. I never knew so fully until then what 'God so loved the world' meant, and I am quite sure my precious mother learnt more of the love of God for the perishing world in that one hour than in all her life before."

These words reveal one of the secrets of Hudson Taylor's power. He was a big human, with a large and tender heart. Though believing in self-denial, and practising it, he was no cold-blooded ascetic. He could endure hardness as a good soldier of Jesus Christ, and expect others to do so too, but he never lost sight of, nor despised, the emotional element in men and women.

For five and a half months the *Dumfries* was his home, and during all this time he and the ship's company were cut off from the world without, for the vessel never touched land. The Cape of Good Hope was rounded in December; the nearest point to Australia, one hundred and twenty miles away, was reached on January 5; and the vessel finally dropped anchor at Woosung, ten miles from Shanghai, on March 1, 1854.

The voyage had been rich in experience. It had opened with a prolonged and terrific storm, during which a watery grave for the ship and crew seemed inevitable. But by dint of great daring the Captain managed, as by a miracle, to clear some dangerous rocks off the Welsh coast, but only by the ship's length. Later on a dead calm, with swift currents running towards sunken reefs, constituted an even greater peril. "In a storm," wrote Hudson Taylor, "the ship is to some extent manageable, but becalmed one can do nothing; the Lord must do all." And so in storm and calm alike he learnt afresh the power of prayer, and the presence of Him who holds the winds and waves in the hollow of His hands.

And there were perils other than physical that Hudson Taylor was saved from on that voyage. The peril, for instance, of mistaking presumption for faith. How many have made shipwreck through despising God's appointed means, as though these were in conflict with trust in God! On this point Hudson Taylor, that man of faith, must speak for himself:

> "I was a very young believer, and had not sufficient faith in God to see Him in and through the use of means. I had felt it a duty to comply with the earnest wish of my beloved and honoured mother, and for her sake to procure a swimming-belt. But in my own soul I felt as if I could not simply trust in God while I had this swimming-belt, and my heart had no rest until on that night, during the storm off the Welsh coast, after all hope of being saved was gone, I had given it away. Then I had perfect peace, and strange to say put several light things together, likely to float at the time we struck, without any thought of inconsistency or scruple.
>
> "Ever since I have seen clearly the mistake I made; a mistake that is very common in these days, when erroneous teaching on faith-healing does much harm, misleading some as to the purposes of God, shaking the faith of others, and distressing the minds of many. The use of means ought not to lessen our faith in God, and our faith in God ought not to hinder our using whatever means He has given us for the accomplishment of His own purposes.... After the storm was over, the question was settled for me through the prayerful study of the Scriptures. God gave me then to see my mistake, probably to deliver me from a great deal of trouble on similar questions now so constantly raised."

Here we see that sane and healthy balance of judgment and character which made Hudson Taylor such a spiritual and practical builder. In this he was like the Apostle Paul, who, when shipwrecked, could say, "Sirs, be of good cheer, for I believe God," and yet, at the same time, warned the centurion when the sailors sought to desert the vessel, "Except these abide in the ship ye cannot be saved." To Paul the technical help the sailors alone could give was not inconsistent with faith in God.

As already mentioned, Hudson Taylor had reached Woosung, on Wednesday, March 1, 1854. But it was not until 5 P.M. on the same day that he landed at Shanghai, a stranger in a strange land. Inevitably it was a day of deep and varied emotions.

"My feelings on stepping ashore," he wrote, "I cannot attempt to describe. My heart felt as though it had not room and must burst its bonds, while tears of gratitude and thankfulness fell from my eyes."

But there were stem and sobering facts to face, and that without delay, for the day was already far spent. He had landed unwelcomed, for there was no one to meet him, nor had he any friends anywhere. This was the more serious since he had learned from the pilot that England was on the brink of the Crimean War, that Shanghai was in the hands of rebels, that the city was invested by an imperial army of fifty thousand men, that food was at famine prices, and that the cost of the dollar had already risen from four to nearly seven shillings, and was still soaring no one knew whither.

These were not encouraging prospects for a lonely youth, not yet twenty-two years of age. But as he had three letters of introduction, he made immediate inquiries concerning those to whom they were addressed. He learned that one of these was dead, another had left for America, but happily the third, Dr. Medhurst, of the London Missionary Society, was still in Shanghai.

Not without some difficulty he found his way to the London Missionary Society's compound, which was more than a mile distant. But though Dr. and Mrs. Medhurst had left for the British Consulate, as their premises were contiguous to the fighting, he was warmly welcomed by Mr. Edkin, Dr. Lockhart, and Mr. Alexander Wylie.

To the new arrival and to the older workers alike the situation was delicate and trying. It was quite impossible then to find premises, or even lodgings, in the foreign settlement, and daily fighting was taking place outside. It seemed altogether inopportune that the pioneer of a new and unproved organization should arrive upon the scenes just then, and Hudson Taylor must have felt it so. But Dr. Lockhart most kindly took him in, as a paying guest, and introduced him to Mr. and Mrs. Muirhead, of the London Missionary Society, and to Mr. and Mrs. Burdon, of the Church Missionary Society. These were all mighty men, as their subsequent record proves, and in welcoming this young and unknown stranger they were entertaining one of God's angels unawares.

But to Hudson Taylor his condition of impotence and dependence was a painful discipline. Unable to speak to the people, he was yet a dumb witness of their misery. The guns could be heard all night, fighting could be seen from his window, while the horrors of a siege, and the wild licence of the soldiery, were all too much in evidence. All his efforts to secure rooms in the Chinese part of the settlement hopelessly failed, so that the only thing he could do was to pray, and give himself to the study of the language.

The outlook was dark indeed. No one could say when the situation would improve, while the cost of living was becoming prohibitive. Coal, for instance, was £10 a ton, and the weather was bitterly cold. He had not brought much money with him, as he expected a letter of credit from the Society to be awaiting his arrival. But there was no letter! It was contrary to his principles to be burdensome to others, but as fugitive Chinese were paying £10 a month for two or three rooms, what could he do with a slender purse and no remittance to hand? It was a painful initiation to his missionary career, and, as he wrote home, "Satan came in like a flood; but there was One who lifted up a standard against him."

VIII

PERPLEXED, BUT NOT IN DESPAIR

H UDSON TAYLOR had reached his desired destination, but it was no haven of rest. Difficulties he had expected, but the reality was beyond all expectation. Active opposition frequently stimulates courage, but to find oneself an embarrassment to others can hardly fail to dishearten.

For the first six months he was obliged to remain as Dr. Lockhart's paying guest, and though the Doctor was kindness itself, his position was unenviable. He was an unknown youth, and his Society laid itself open to serious criticism. He was allowed an income of only £80 a year. He could not rent a house in the Settlement under £120 per annum! His Society would not grant him discretionary powers, and though they gave him a letter of credit in case of emergencies, before he had been six months in the land they passed a resolution saying that bills exceeding £40 per quarter would not be honoured.

It was painful to find that the Society under which he laboured was becoming an object of ridicule in Shanghai, and that even the sympathetic friend who cashed his bills spoke scathingly of it. Unjust criticism he never feared, but this he knew was too well deserved, and so it hurt.

Mail after mail arrived from home with no adequate response to his representations, and to his shame and perplexity he heard from outside sources that new workers were on their way, and were looking to him for a welcome and a home. These reinforcements were Dr. and Mrs. Parker with three children, and yet the Society had sent him neither information nor instructions.

Not long after his arrival in Shanghai the battle at Muddy Flat was fought, when a small Anglo-American force defeated some fifty thousand imperial troops. This naturally made it perilous for foreigners to move outside the settlement, but none the less he felt he could no longer be beholden to his friends, and so he rented a ramshackle Chinese house near the Chinese city. His was now a position full of peril, where sleep was next to impossible, for his house was at times not only struck with gunshot, but even by cannon-ball. Still, he could afford no other, and so for several months he held on there. Each night the rude plank bridge between himself and the settlement was removed, and so he slept, or tried to sleep, with his swimming belt ever at hand, and a small light burning in case of emergencies.

It was but natural that such a strain should tell upon him, and there are references in his letters of this period to sickness and to nervous irritability. But he assiduously continued at his study of the language, and at such evangelistic work as was possible. Freely he mingled with the people, at one time interviewing a rebel chief in an effort to prevent bloodshed, and shirking no risk to do what he could to relieve the wounded. Even under these conditions he could see the humorous side of things and could and did "burst into a fit of laughter, most inappropriate to the occasion."

But at times he was tempted to faint, yet was encouraged by considering the example of Him at whose command he had come.

> "Our dear Redeemer," he wrote, "had not where to lay His head. I have never yet been placed in that extremity. One who is really leaning on the Beloved finds it always possible to say, 'I will fear no evil, for Thou art with me.' But I am so apt, like Peter, to take my eyes off the one Object and look at the waves and winds.... Oh, for more stability!"

"Temptations when first we meet them," wrote Bunyan, "are as the lion that roared upon Samson, but if we overcome them, the next time we see them we shall find a nest of honey within." And this Hudson Taylor was finding. Out of the eater was coming forth meat. "Though in some ways," he wrote, "I never passed a more anxious month in my life, I have never felt so conscious of God's presence with me."

It is easy now to look back and see that these trials were preparing him for his post of leadership in days to come. By the things which he suffered he was being fitted for watching over the interests of others, and gaining a power to sympathize with lonely workers up country. But the iron was entering into his soul, and he felt compelled to send a formally worded protest to his own Society concerning their neglect.

When the house next door had been burnt to the ground, and his own belongings destroyed also, he, greatly daring, took one of the London Missionary Society's houses, which had suddenly become vacant, at the rent of £120 per year. And yet after he had paid only the first instalment he had less than enough for one week's living expenses in hand.

And these premises were secured none too soon, for two days later Dr. Parker and family arrived. It was with some consternation he learned that they also only had a few dollars with them for immediate use. But remittances were expected, in fact should have been waiting Dr. Parker's arrival. But though mails, posted in England three months after the Parkers had sailed, arrived ere long, they brought no remittance, nor even any mention of money! And yet Hudson Taylor had been criticized at Shanghai, by those who did not know the facts, for not making more adequate provision for the comforts of a family with little children!

All this was trying enough, but when his Society's magazine at home began to publish statements critical of those who were befriending him in Shanghai, he felt he had no option but to remonstrate. It was a painful duty, but it was done with firmness, and yet with much humility, as the following extracts from his correspondence show:

Concerning what was published in *The Gleaner* he wrote:

> "From the December *Gleaner* (I think it was) I see you have no one to revise the sheets, or that monstrous mass of absurdities printed as my communication could never have been passed. Better have no *Gleaner* at all, than send out such a tissue of

nonsense, to make the Society and its agents a laughing stock to all who see it.... You should not voluntarily irritate those who are more thoughtful for the shelter and support of your missionaries than the Society which sends them out seems to be."

In another letter he writes quite frankly telling the Committee at home of his painful dismay at finding no reference to finance in mail after mail, acquainting them with the inadequate preparations he had made for the welcome of the Parkers, their lack of funds, and the criticisms he had suffered in consequence, of how his mouth was closed against explanations, and also of the kindnesses he had received from friends in Shanghai. He then proceeds:

"I trust you will not deem it unkind or disrespectful of me to write thus. For though I feel these things and feel them keenly, were it not for the sake of others and the good of the Society, I would pass them over in silence. To do this, however, would be unfaithfulness on my part. For not only is it morally wrong and thoughtless in the extreme to act as the Society has acted towards Dr. Parker, but you must surely see that men who can quadruple their salary by professional practice, or double it by taking a clerk's berth, will not be likely, if they find themselves totally unprovided for, to continue in the service of the Society....

"I may add that a vacant post at £200 a year, the whole duties of which would not occupy two hours in the evening, did look inviting to me at a time when I had been obliged to incur a responsibility of £120 for rent, and a Resolution upon my last letter to the Committee informed me that missionaries drawing more than was authorized would not have their bills honoured by the Society.

"Now you cannot but see, I am sure, what evidence this is of gross neglect. We do, at any rate. And while we both cherish the warmest and most affectionate regard for many members of the Committee personally, and especially for the Secretaries, we cannot but feel the Society has acted disgracefully."

In another letter, after referring again to the woeful lack of business-like methods in the management of the Society's affairs, and the folly of not allowing the workers on the field discretion as to the day on which letters of credit should be cashed, when the price of silver was constantly undergoing rapid and great variations, he concludes with the following words, almost of apology:

> "If I have spoken too warmly, forgive me; and remember I am only a weak brother, in pecuniary anxiety and embarrassment, as well as in a position of great peril, entirely isolated from Christian sympathy, communion, and friendship; and that these things and sickness, and spiritual conflict with the adversary of souls, are at times almost more than I can bear. Rest assured Satan does not let those pass without trial and temptation whose sole object and desire is the overthrow of his kingdom; but, thank God, He does not suffer him to have his own way, but strengthens His servants for the conflict. But notwithstanding, I feel ready to faint sometimes."

Such letters were not written before he had suffered long and silently, and then only because the honour of his Master and of the Society was at stake. Yet all these provocations did not hinder him from using to the limits of his ability every opportunity for useful service which came his way. Not only did he labour in Shanghai, but, when possible, he with others of the missionary community itinerated in the environs of the city, though such work was beset by many dangers.

IX

IN JOURNEYINGS OFT

THOUGH FEELING at times a sense of utter isolation and helplessness, and though tried by cold and even hunger, with watchings and sleepless nights, there was one thing Hudson Taylor would not do, and that was he would never allow adversity to paralyse his activities. When most beset by trial his policy was advance. And so, despite the harassing failure of the friends at home, he showed his faith in God by aggressive evangelism. "Useful we must and will be, if the Lord bless us, at any cost," was his resolve.

And so, within a few weeks of Dr. Parker's arrival, we find him commencing a series of evangelistic journeys into areas seldom or never visited before by Protestant missionaries. Sometimes he was alone, sometimes accompanied by Dr. Parker, at other times he went in company with senior workers of other Societies, such as Mr. Edkin and Mr. Burdon. Without attempting to follow in detail his many itinerations, it must suffice to say that between December, 1854, and the autumn of 1855, he had made no fewer than eight longer and shorter journeys, one of these extending to nearly two hundred miles up the southern bank of the river Yangtse. On this occasion he came to within sixty miles of Chinkiang, travelled in all nearly five hundred miles, entered no fewer than fifty-eight cities, towns and villages, fifty-one of which had never been visited before by preachers of the Gospel. In all this work the British and Foreign Bible Society supplied him with Scriptures, and met in part his travelling expenses, which, as he was apparently forgotten by his own Society, came as a very welcome assistance.

Such journeys in those days were full of hazard. As foreigners had enlisted themselves on both sides in the rebellion, he was liable at any time to be seized and roughly handled, if not even killed, by an infuriated and suspicious people. "But," he wrote, "the Word of God *must* go, and we must not be hindered by slight obstacles in the way of its dissemination." What these "slight obstacles" were may, in part, be gathered by the following paragraphs. On one of his journeys he was arrested, when on an eminence, by the smoke of a vast conflagration. This was nothing less than Shanghai in flames, and whether the foreign settlement was involved with the Chinese city, he did not know. It was a terrible journey home. Poor defenceless men were constantly appealing to him for protection, and these he frequently saw beheaded before his eyes. But happily the Shanghai foreign settlements had been spared, for the Imperialists had been too busy in slaughtering their own countrymen.

> "Shanghai," he wrote, referring to the Chinese city, "is now in peace, but it is like the peace of death. Two thousand people at the very least have perished, and the tortures some of the victims have undergone cannot have been exceeded by the worst barbarities of the Inquisition. The city is little more than a mass of ruins."

On another occasion, in the spring of 1855, he and Mr. Burdon set out to visit a group of islands situated in the great mouth of the Yangtse River, of which Tsungming and Haimen were the largest and most important. After some time had been spent evangelizing these islands and in visting Langshan, or Wealthy Mountain, a resort famous for pilgrim devotees, they determined to visit the influential city of Tungchow.

The day was dull and wet, and they had an inward persuasion that serious opposition awaited their assault upon this stronghold of the adversary. Further, their Chinese teachers sought to dissuade them, and a friendly stranger on the road warned them against the Tungchow Militia. Their servants, too, were frightened, and requested and received permission to go back. But the hearts of these two workers were fixed, and their faces set like flints; whether it meant bonds, imprisonment, or death, they were determined that that city should no longer be left without the offer of salvation.

"Never was I so happy in speaking of the love of God and of the atonement of Jesus Christ," wrote Hudson Taylor concerning his efforts by the way. But as he and his friend approached the western suburbs of the city, the prayer of the early Christians came aptly into Hudson Taylor's mind. "And now, Lord, behold their threatenings, and grant unto Thy servants that with all boldness they may speak Thy Word."

No prayer could have been more timely, for before the city gate was reached a tall and powerful man, made ten times fiercer by partial intoxication, seized Mr. Burdon by the shoulders, while a dozen more brutal men surrounded them both and violently hustled them forward. Soon the intoxicated giant became Hudson Taylor's principal tormentor, seizing him by the hair, almost choking him, and so roughly handling him that he all but fainted. Yet despite this violence they still sought to distribute their Christian literature, not knowing whether they might have another opportunity. But the mad rage of their chief persecutor, who called for manacles, at length compelled them to desist. Some were for dragging them before the Mandarin, some were for killing them on the spot. Although the long and weary streets seemed to have no end, the Yamen was at length reached, when both Hudson Taylor and his friend were glad to lean against the wall, bathed in perspiration, exhausted, and with their tongues cleaving to the roofs of their mouths.

In the good providence of God the official had once been Taotai of Shanghai, and knew the importance of treating foreigners with respect. Not only did he show them deference, but he listened to their message, and accepted a copy of the New Testament and other books. This was a welcome opening, and they availed themselves of it by requesting permission to see the city and distribute their books. This was granted, and their books were distributed unmolested, and they left the city quite in state. Though battered and weary it was with grateful hearts they reached their boats in safety, and thanked God for the labours and the mercies of a trying day.

Such journeyings as these, with their vision of the needy multitude, turned Hudson Taylor's mind more and more from the settled ports to the unreached millions of the interior. He was unable to disregard the call of those vast unevangelized regions.

> "Wherever one goes," he wrote, "cities, towns, and villages just teem with inhabitants, few of whom have ever heard the only Name under Heaven given among men whereby we must be saved. Just to visit them, give away portions of Scripture and tracts, and after preaching a few times, pass on to other places, seems almost like doing nothing for the people. And yet unless this course is adopted how are those further on ever to hear at all. We see no fruit at present, and it needs strong faith to keep one's heart from sinking; besides which, I have felt a degree of nervousness since we were so roughly treated in Tungchow, which is quite a new experience, a feeling which is not lessened by being quite alone. I remember, however, His faithful promise, 'they that sow in tears shall reap in joy.'"

And so the call of the interior was strengthened, and out of one of those journeys, a journey to Ningpo, unexpected developments arose. It was quite clear that the Society at home was not prepared to spend anything on bricks and mortar, and in consequence Dr. Parker had no scope in Shanghai for medical work. Indeed, so pressed were they for room that Hudson Taylor had to make his bedroom do for a study both for himself and Dr. Parker, so that he had no place for a moment's privacy. But out of this journey to Ningpo God's way became clear, for Ningpo was the only open port without a doctor, and the missionary community there invited Dr. Parker to open a hospital, and promised the necessary financial support for such an undertaking.

And just when this opening for Dr. Parker opportunely appeared, Hudson Taylor was himself offered a house within the Chinese city of Shanghai, after having long sought for one in vain, and with this opening in the Chinese city came other changes too, such as the adoption of the Chinese dress.

> "I parted from Dr. Parker last night," he wrote on August 28, 1855, "and am now alone for the first time in the interior in Chinese costume.... The very evening before we left Shanghai I obtained a house in the native city for quite a moderate rent. From repeated disappointments I had quite given up the hope of getting one. I thought I was going to be houseless and homeless for the time being. How true it is, 'Man's extremity is God's opportunity.' The change from a large household, two families beside myself, to living quite alone will, no doubt, have its trials, but I hope to be rewarded by increasing fluency in the language leading to greater usefulness."

We have now reached an important stage in Hudson Taylor's life. The way for residence and work in the foreign settlement at Shanghai had been closed by the definite decision of the Society he represented, and by their failure to send out adequate supplies. This decision, together with his own experiences, had caused him to set his eyes as never before towards work in the interior, and for this purpose he had adopted the Chinese dress. This was a bigger step than appears upon the surface. The sneers of the European community, and the disfavour of some of the missionary body, which pained him even more, helped to inaugurate a new departure. But the larger liberty, and the greater freedom, he experienced, in moving about among the people in the land of his adoption, were not only an abundant compensation for what he suffered, but a confirmation of the wisdom of the decision.

And it was during his first months in the Chinese city that he was rejoiced beyond measure by his first convert's request for baptism. "If one soul is worth worlds," he wrote to his mother, "am I not abundantly repaid, and are not you too?"

But there was further encouragement. Mr. W. T. Berger, who was to be among the staunchest and most generous of his friends at home, had begun to take an interest in his work, and to send him financial aid. So here he rejoiced in the beginnings of his spiritual harvest, and in God opening up to him of a new way of supplies.

That he was being led we can see now, but to him much was dark, and he still had to learn to walk alone with God. "The future is a ravelling maze," he wrote, "but my path has always been made plain just one step at a time. I must wait on God, and trust in Him, and all will be well."

X

A MEMORABLE FRIENDSHIP

OR THE best part of two years Hudson Taylor had been all alone in the deepest things of his life. In the midst of many perplexing and harassing experiences he had had no one to whom he could, without reserve, unburden his heart. He had landed in China to find his liberty curtailed by civil war; he had found himself, much against his inclination, dependent upon the hospitality of others; he had been embarrassed almost beyond measure by the negligence of his Society at home; and he had smarted under the undeserved criticism of those to whom he could not reveal the real facts. All of this, and much more, he had had to endure without the comfort of a kindred spirit to sympathize with him. This had doubtless shut him up as never before to God alone, and had thus fortified his soul against future days of battle. But it was all a distressing discipline to one who ardently craved for fellowship.

"Faith," it has been said, "is a spiritual energy of a peculiarly social order. It is sensitive to the presence or absence of sympathy. To be absolutely and unintermittently confident of what no one else believes is so difficult as to be wellnigh impossible, while trust in God is easy when one lives among the trustful." And Hudson Taylor as a pioneer, in a new order of missionary activities, had to stand much alone. But God's time was drawing near when he was to find the fellowship he craved. But, for the present, he continued in his lonely lot with determined patience.

The zeal of God's house consumed him, and great joy flooded his soul when an opening seemed to present itself of securing a settlement in inland China. During a visit to the island of Tsungming he was unexpectedly prospered in renting a house, and here, while he rejoiced with trembling, he settled and commenced medical work. The island gave him a parish of one million souls, forty miles away from Shanghai, the nearest port. It was hard to say which emotion predominated, the heavy burden of responsibility in being the only light-bearer among so many, or joy for such an opportunity. But his success in relieving pain, and curing the sick, soon made the local doctors and druggists look upon him as a serious rival. Their trade, like that of the silversmiths at Ephesus, was in peril, and this intruder must be expelled at any price.

But week after week passed by, and good work was being accomplished. Three persons, at least, testified to their faith in Christ, and there were other hopeful inquirers. But after six happy though anxious weeks a bolt from the blue fell. He was stunned to receive a summons to appear before the British Consul to answer for the offence of residing away from a treaty port. There was nothing for it but to present himself before that dignitary, to find that he was forbidden, under penalty of a fine of five hundred dollars, and possible deportation if he persisted, to live so far away. It was a terrible blow and a bitter disappointment.

> "My heart is sad, sad, sad," he wrote to his mother. "I do not want to be a hireling who flees when the wolf is near. I want to know the Lord's Will, and have grace to do it, even if it result in expatriation."

At first he felt he could not yield without a protest, and he courteously pointed out to the Consul that French Roman Catholic priests, under the protection of France, were actually living on the island. Why should not he enjoy the privileges of "the most favoured nation" clause? The Consul acknowledged the cogency of this argument, but said that to discuss the point was beyond his province. The only way was to appeal to Sir John Bowring, the British minister.

This, he was quite prepared to do, if opportunity offered, not for his own sake only, but for the sake of all Protestant missionary work in China. Meanwhile he wrote to his Society at home to ask if they would be willing to pay the fine of $500, should that penalty be inflicted, for he was quite prepared to go inland again. And more than that, he asked if they would approve of his "giving up all claim to Consular protection," though this might subject him to the cruelties of Chinese law. He was by no means ignorant of the indignities, the treacheries, and the sufferings that this might entail, but he was burdened with the spiritual need of the people, and counted not his life dear unto himself if he might but minister to them.

It was at this juncture that he was brought into touch with the apostolic missionary William Burns, whose wide experience as an evangelist in the Home countries, and in China, made him just the friend and counsellor he so sorely needed. And William Burns found in Hudson Taylor a man after his own heart, and for seven months they clave together as kindred souls and fellow-labourers. "Never had I had such a spiritual father as Mr. Burns," he wrote years afterwards; "never had I known such holy, happy intercourse." The hungry heart was satisfied.

For the next three months these two travelled together in the neighbourhood of Shanghai, availing themselves of the many waterways of Kiangsu, and living on boats. Each had his own boat for the sake of privacy, but they journeyed in company, preaching the Gospel in the cities, towns, and busy market-places during the day, and retiring to their boats at night for rest and refreshment. Thus they enjoyed constant fellowship in the work of the Gospel, and in the things of the spirit.

"A good boat," wrote Hudson Taylor, "costing about two shillings a day, gives me a nice room to myself, one in front for my servant to sleep in, used in the day time for receiving guests, and a cabin behind for my teacher, as well as a place for cooking, storing books, etc. My tiny room has an oyster-shell window that gives light while it prevents people peeping, a table at which I write and take meals... a locker on which my bed is spread at night... and a seat round the remaining space, so that two visitors, or even three, can be accommodated. For family worship we open the doors in front and behind my cabin, and then the boat people, teachers, servants, and Mr. Burns can join in the service."

William Burns was a man who said that "God's presence or absence alone distinguishes places to me." Life with such a man of God was just what Hudson Taylor desired and needed, and to be able to discuss with him the practical problems of the evangelization of China, not as academic questions, but as living and everyday issues, was a liberal education.

The three months together in Mid-China were followed by four months together in South China, at Swatow. This was a big change to Hudson Taylor, and entailed the learning of a new dialect. But a Christian captain had so powerfully represented the spiritual needs of Swatow, and offered a free passage thither, that Hudson Taylor and William Burns had each felt the call, and, as they had not taken counsel together, had each been prepared to respond although it appeared to demand the pain of separation. It was only when Hudson Taylor, with tears in his eyes, told his friend that God had called him south that he found that William Burns had been passing through a similar experience.

Swatow was notorious as a centre of the opium trade, and of the hateful coolie traffic, and here foreigners, though it was not an open port, had bought land and built houses. The opium trade alone was worth a quarter of a million sterling monthly. And in this place, a place of violence and vice, there was no witness for Christ, the nearest missionary being one hundred and fifty miles away.

Early in March these two keen souls left Shanghai in Captain Bowers' steamer, and were thankful, when Swatow was reached, to secure so much as a bare room over an incense shop for residence. For some time it appeared impossible to gain a foothold, so any *pied-à-terre* was welcome, even these rude quarters, which had to be entered through a trap-door in the floor, and where there was nothing but naked tiles between them and the blazing sun.

> "Not easily shall I forget," wrote Hudson Taylor, "the long hot summer months in that oven-like place, where towards the eaves one could touch the heated tiles with one's hand. More room or better accommodation it was impossible to obtain."

It was not strange that living in such a veritable oven for the study of the language, Hudson Taylor should find his health affected. And there were other trials as well. He was no stranger to hardship, as we have seen, and yet he wrote of Swatow:

> "I think I never was in such a wicked place." And again: "It is much more difficult to itinerate here than it was around Shanghai.... It is an entirely new line of things to me and requires far more faith and self-denial than anything I have ever known." And again: "The hatred and contempt of the Cantonese was very painful, 'foreign devil,' 'foreign dog,' or 'foreign pig,' being the commonest appellations; but all this led us into deeper fellowship than I had ever known before with Him Who was 'despised and rejected of men.'"

From one so inured to roughing it, and so willing to endure hardness, these words meant much. But he felt that God was training him for something, though he knew not what, and was content.

In the height of summer, an official whom Chinese doctors could not aid, but who had been healed through Hudson Taylor's ministry, gratefully offered to help them rent a house. This was indeed welcome news, not only because it met a pressing personal need, but because it afforded a prospect of wider usefulness. And so, in order to start medical work on a larger scale, Hudson Taylor agreed to go to Shanghai to fetch his medical equipment. As a free passage was offered him for this purpose, he set forth with a glad heart, thankful also for a short sea trip, as the almost insufferable heat of their small attic had injuriously affected his health. But little did he know when he said farewell to his friend William Burns, that he would never see his face again.

Unknown to both, dark clouds of war were shortly to gather in the south, and were to burst into an armed conflict that was to last for years. This was occasioned by the Chinese Government seizing the lorcha *Arrow,* which, while flying the British flag, but without authorization, was engaged in smuggling opium. After fruitless negotiations Canton was bombarded by the British in October, 1856, and peace was not ratified until 1860. It is a humiliating chapter in the history of Anglo-Chinese relations, and would never have been written but for haste and a haughty spirit. And William Burns was to be seized as a prisoner and sent under escort to Canton, some thirty-one days' journey away, but happily before the passions of the people had been inflamed against the British by the war.

But all this was unknown when Hudson Taylor and William Burns bid one another farewell in July, hoping for a speedy reunion. But though they never met again on earth, these seven months of friendship and fellowship had done their work, and Hudson Taylor subsequently wrote:

> "Those happy months were an unspeakable joy and comfort to me. His love for the Word was delightful, and his holy reverential life and constant communings with God made fellowship with him satisfying to the deep cravings of my heart. His accounts of revival work and of persecutions in Canada, Dublin, and Southern China were most instructive as well as interesting; for with true spiritual insight he often pointed out God's purpose in trial in a way that made all life assume quite a new aspect and value. His views especially about evangelism as the great work of the Church, and the order of lay-evangelists as a lost order that Scripture required to be restored, were seed thoughts which were to prove fruitful in the subsequent organization of the China Inland Mission."

But Hudson Taylor was only separated from William Burns to find that God had another rich gift in store, the gift of the love of a woman whose price was far above rubies, and who was to do him "good and not evil, all the days of her life." But of this he knew nothing then, and of all things it seemed the most improbable. Yet is it true in God's economy:

> "That looking backward through our tears,
> With vision of maturer scope,
> How often one dead joy appears
> The platform of some brighter hope."

XI

LOVE TRIUMPHANT

WHEN HUDSON Taylor left Swatow all he had anticipated was a brief absence from William Burns. He was to encounter, however, a strange succession of disappointments, and to find himself thwarted at every turn. Faith and courage were to be tested to the uttermost. He did not, could not see the wealthy place towards which all was leading.

When the eager traveller reached Shanghai he learned to his dismay that the whole of his medical outfit had been destroyed by fire. This was calamity number one. As the cost of a new equipment was prohibitive in Shanghai, he set out for Ningpo, hoping Dr. Parker would have some drugs to spare. But he was robbed and deserted on the road by his own servant, and learned the deep significance of the Apostle's words: "In perils of robbers, in perils from the Gentiles, in perils of the city, in perils of the wilderness." This was calamity number two.

Then when Ningpo was reached and the drugs obtained, a month later than he expected, he was delayed on the return journey by the sickness of others. Here was calamity number three.

But what seemed worst of all was the news, just as he was boarding the steamer for Swatow, that William Burns had been seized by Chinese and sent under escort to Canton, and, further, that the British authorities had forbidden any attempt to reoccupy Swatow. What could these misfortunes mean? Why all these fruitless journeyings? What lay behind God's mysterious dealings? But there were good reasons why he should not go south, and better reasons why he should remain north.

> "Be not amazed at life; 'tis still
> The mode of God with His elect.
> Their hopes exactly to fulfil.
> In times and ways they least expect."

This truth Hudson Taylor was to prove, but only by passing through fire and water. When news came later that the British had bombarded Canton, and then that war had been declared, he recognised the wisdom and the kindness which had blocked his path. And when in Ningpo he met the woman whose love seemed countless gain, he saw the loving Hand which had detained him in the north. But his Eden was fenced in with apparently insurmountable barriers. He could only acknowledge God in all His ways, and trust Him to direct his paths. And this he literally did, come rough, come smooth.

SCRIPTURE TESTIMONY

Disciples are devoted to Christ above anything or anyone

MATTHEW 4:20-22 · MATTHEW 16:24-25 · MARK 1:19-20 · MARK 8:31-38 · MARK 10:28 · LUKE 9:23-27 · LUKE 9:57-62 · LUKE 14:25-35

When he had been robbed and deserted on the road to Ningpo, he still sought first to preach Christ. He speaks of feeling condemned for being anxious about his lost belongings, and not more concerned for the lost state of those around. Though so exhausted by lack of food, by want of sleep, and by sheer physical fatigue as to faint by the roadside, he only regained consciousness to continue his witness for Christ. Literally he sought first the things of God, and believing that God would not fail to deliver him, he bade some interested Chinese observe how God would come to his aid. So real was the sense of God's presence that at times, though utterly weary, he said "the road was almost forgotten," and "sweet tears of mingled joy and sorrow flowed freely." As the sceptic David Hume said of Dr. John Brown: "He spoke as if Jesus Christ was at his elbow!" And he believed He was.

Improbable as it appeared in a land where one man's misfortune is considered another man's opportunity, he was enabled, though without money, to secure a passage to Shanghai, a friendly Chinese standing security should he fail to recoup the boatman at his destination. He trusted and proved God in this time of dire need, and the first mail to reach him in Shanghai after his return brought him a gift of £40 from Mr. and Mrs. Berger, as a token of their love! Posted in England long before the robbery, in fact, before he had left Swatow, it came as a heart-moving reminder that God had foreseen and had provided.

And, though he did not learn the fact till long afterward, his letters home, telling his people that he did not purpose prosecuting his servant, but rather to seek to overcome his evil by good, fell into the hands of George Müller, and secured him as a lifelong friend of the Mission that was yet to be.

But the keenest and most searching discipline of all was still before him, and was connected with his affection for the woman of his choice. In Ningpo, where, after a brief period in Shanghai, he had found his sphere of labour, lived Maria Dyer, who awakened in his heart all that love of which his ardent nature was capable. In every way she answered to his ideal of a chosen helpmeet, and yet, when he revealed his hopes, he received a cold and blank refusal.

His fervent love, together with a deep conviction that God was in it, still urged him to hope on. He did not know, and could not know, that her negative had been dictated by another to whom, for the time being, she was subject.

Maria Dyer was a bright and winsome girl, not yet of age, the daughter of Samuel Dyer of the London Missionary Society. This Mr. Dyer, though educated at Cambridge for the Bar, had, as early as 1827, dedicated himself to God for work among the Chinese, amongst whom he laboured for sixteen years until his death. Gifted and devoted beyond many, he was consumed with a passion for the salvation of the Chinese. "If I thought anything could prevent my dying for China, the thought would crush me," he had once written. Such words, and others like them, reveal the man he was, and his daughter was possessed of a like spirit. It was no wonder Hudson Taylor loved her.

Orphaned in early life, Maria Dyer, with her elder sister, Burella, who married the Rev. J. S. Burden (later the Bishop of Victoria, Hongkong), joined Miss Aldersey at Ningpo in the first girls' school opened by missionaries in China. Fluent in the language from birth, Maria Dyer was well adapted for this work, and in Miss Aldersey she had as chief a remarkable and commanding personality. Miss Aldersey had been a student of Chinese under Dr. Robert Morrison during his first and only furlough, and was the first single woman to go to China as a missionary. So profound an impression did she make upon the Chinese that they believed the British Consul took his commands from her, a belief encouraged by the fact that the reigning British soverign—Queen Victoria —was a woman. Hudson Taylor and Maria Dyer were to find in her a formidable opponent to their love affairs.

For some reason Miss Aldersey had taken a violent prejudice against Hudson Taylor. She disliked his adoption of the Chinese dress; she disapproved of his methods of work. Another resident in Ningpo, Dr. W. A. P. Martin, who afterwards learned his worth, regarded Hudson Taylor as "a mystic absorbed in religious dreams, waiting to have his work revealed; not idle, but aimless." He had no home, no settled income, no prospects, and he represented no Society, for he had severed his connection with the Chinese Evangelization Society. These were all good and adequate reasons, in Miss Aldersey's eyes, to prove he had no right to think of marriage. She probably forgot that the apostles were poor, and that some at least had "no certain dwelling place." But prejudice, especially with so determined a woman, was a formidable force, and many painful, almost incredible statements began to gain circulation. All Miss Aldersey's powerful influence was set to frustrate Hudson Taylor's hopes of winning Maria Dyer.

This was a period of acutest suffering. Miss Aldersey had Maria Dyer's ear, and she contrived that Hudson Taylor should not meet her. Honour and chivalry forbade him to write again, since he had already been denied that approach. God alone was his hope. He knew that he must conquer through prayer or fail. Little did he realize that Maria Dyer herself was suffering as keenly as he himself. Not yet of age, and with her guardian in England, she was overborne by Miss Aldersey's powerful personality.

But love will out, and circumstances at long last let Hudson Taylor see the lie of the land, and from Maria Dyer he obtained permission to write to her guardian, her uncle Mr. Tam, in England. This was in July, 1857, but no reply could be expected before the end of November. The prospect did not appear hopeful, for both knew that Miss Aldersey would leave no stone unturned to bias Mr. Tam's mind. The months of waiting which ensued could not fail to be a time of acute and anxious suspense.

Nor was this all, for in other ways Hudson Taylor was at that period passing through the refiner's fire, and being purged as gold and silver. One such momentous experience was the severance of his connection with the Society which had sent him out to China. For many months he had been deeply pained and exercised by the fact that the Chinese Evangelization Society was frequently in debt, and that the bills which he and others were instructed to draw were met with borrowed money. God's word, "Owe no man anything," was to him unmistakably definite, and to borrow money was therefore tantamount to a confession that man was determined to obtain what God had withheld.

> "Could that which was wrong for one Christian to do," he wrote, "be right for an association of Christians? I could not think that God was poor, that He was short of resources, or unwilling to supply any want of whatever work was really His."

The logic of this seemed unanswerable, and since he was unable, after a long correspondence, to bring the Society to his way of thinking, he felt compelled, to satisfy his conscience, to sever his connection with them, though without any breach of love and goodwill. He continued to send home his journal for the Society to publish as before.

There was naturally much that was trying in such a step. He had no desire to become a free-lance, but as he was unordained, and had not completed his medical course, he was not sanguine as to any other Society accepting him. But of one thing he was certain, and that was that God would never leave him, nor forsake him. But he was none the less deeply exercised.

> "I was not at all sure what God would have me do," he subsequently wrote, "or whether He would so meet my need as to

enable me to continue working as before. I had no friends whatever from whom I expected supplies. I did not know what means
the Lord might use, but I was willing to give up all my time to
the service of evangelization among the heathen, if by any means
He would supply the smallest amount on which I could live; and
if He were not pleased to do this, I was prepared to undertake
whatever work might be necessary to supply myself, giving all the
time that could be spared from such a calling to more distinctly
missionary efforts."

It was a severe ordeal, another launching out into the great unknown,
another occasion for stepping out on the promises of God.

"How glad one is now," he wrote, "not only to know, with dear Miss
Havergal, that

> They who trust Him wholly
> Find Him wholly true,

but also, that when we fail to trust Him fully He still remains unchang-
ingly faithful. He is wholly true whether we trust or not. 'If we believe
not, He abideth faithful; He cannot deny Himself.'"

It did not make it less trying that this step of faith had to be taken
just when he was seeking to win the love of Maria Dyer in face of
determined opposition. But he would not win her affection under any
misapprehension, and she was destined to see the worst, and the best,
to see him "as poor, yet making many rich; as having nothing, and yet
possessing all things."

The workings of Hudson Taylor's mind are revealed by those portions
of God's Word which at this time became the rock on which he built.
We all seize upon that which supplies a felt and present need. It is one
day this, and another day that. And it was at this juncture that we find
two scrolls, in Chinese character, hanging over his mantelpiece—*Ebenezer,*
"Hitherto hath the Lord helped us;" and *Jehovah Jireh,* "The Lord will
provide." These selections from Scripture are as windows into his mind,
they mirror forth his thoughts, and they remained as foundations for his
faith. And because he had so many occasions to prove God's gracious

provision, few men have raised more Ebenezers. Some mark the path he
trod during those trying months prior to his marriage.

Late in the autumn of 1857,
while eagerly awaiting the fateful answer from Mr. Tam, a
fellow-missionary, the Rev. John

SCRIPTURE TESTIMONY
God provides exactly what is needed
2 CORINTHIANS 8:15 · PHILIPPIANS 4:19

Quarterman of the American Presbyterian Mission North, was taken
seriously ill with virulent smallpox. Though Hudson Taylor had barely
recovered from sickness himself he gladly volunteered to nurse the
sick man. The disease unhappily proved fatal, though all that devoted
care could do was done. Hudson Taylor himself contracted the same
dread disorder, but escaped with a mild attack through having recently
been vaccinated.

But amid the solemnities of this time one apparently trivial thing
brought him no small comfort. After all it is not the magnitude of an
experience which measures its significance. A cup of water in the desert
is more than gold in a land of plenty. And it was at this time that Hudson
Taylor, having had to destroy the clothing he wore when nursing his
smallpox patient, found himself with a depleted wardrobe, and an empty
exchequer. Had he conserved the funds which came his way he would
have been plentifully supplied, but he had been sharing his all with a
colleague, and had also lent a fellow-missionary the sum of £37. Freely he
had received and freely he had given. But now he was sorely in need of a
new outfit, but his purse was empty.

It was at this juncture that a long-lost box of clothing, which he
had left behind at Swatow fifteen months before, unexpectedly arrived,
bringing him just what he needed. Such timely supplies could not fail
to possess a value far beyond their worth. Their arrival was, he wrote,
"as appropriate as it was remarkable, and brought a sweet sense of the
Father's own providing."

That he was happy to walk thus by faith and not by sight, is evident
from his journal:

"I would not, if I could," he wrote, "be otherwise than as I am—entirely
dependent upon the Lord, and used as a channel to help others."

These words he wrote in November, 1857, on the eve of hearing from Mr. Tam. How he was situated when he penned those words must now be told.

SCRIPTURE TESTIMONY
God's work will not lack God's supply
PHILIPPIANS 4:19

He was daily providing free breakfasts for a number of destitute people, varying from forty to eighty in number. On Saturday, November 4, after having paid all expenses, and having provided for the Sunday, he had not a dollar left. How the needs of Monday would be met he did not know, yet the poor were not warned not to come. The two scrolls over the mantelpiece banished all doubt and fear. And his confidence was not misplaced, for on that very day, a week sooner than had been anticipated, his colleague, Mr. Jones, received a bill for $214.

"Oh, it is sweet," he wrote, "to live thus dependent upon the Lord who never fails."

"How easy it is with money in the pocket and food in the cupboard," he wrote, on another occasion, "to think that one has faith. We need a faith that rests on a great God, and which expects Him to keep His own word, and to do just what He has promised."

On Monday the hungry poor came as before, and it was with eyes filled with gratitude to the God who had met his own need that he supplied the want of the widow and the orphan.

By January 6, 1858, once again the last dollar had been spent, and this time he and Mr. Jones and family had only one cash between them, i.e. the twentieth of a penny.

Meanwhile the fateful letter from Mr. Tarn had arrived, and had brought his cordial consent to the engagement. There was only one request, and that was that Maria Dyer should not marry before she was twenty- one. But this was only a matter of days! Such liberty opened the gates of paradise to both hearts. The pain and the anxiety of the long-sustained suspense gave place to joy and gladness.

"I can scarcely realise, dear Mother," he wrote home, "what has happened; that after all the agony and suspense we have suffered we are not only at liberty to meet and be much with each other, but that within a few days, D.V., we are to be married! God has been good to us."

And it spoke much not only for her love for Hudson Taylor, but also for her faith in God, that, knowing what she did, she did not hold back on financial grounds.

January 20, four days after her twenty-first birthday, had been fixed for the wedding, and here, just a fortnight before, Hudson Taylor and

SCRIPTURE TESTIMONY
God will provide for our daily needs
MATTHEW 6:11

his friend Mr. Jones were reduced to their last cash! And what was more, Maria Dyer was coming to tea, in company with Mrs. Bausum! This was surely the last day on which he would have desired such an emergency to happen. Was he really to be thus put to shame?

"Enough remained in the house to supply a modest breakfast," he wrote, "after which, having neither food for the rest of the day nor money to obtain any, we could only betake ourselves to Him who is a real Father, and cannot forget His children's needs. And you may be sure," he added, "that what was to me the most painful element in the situation, our unpreparedness for the guests who were coming that evening, was specially remembered before Him."

There was no mail due, and no source whence supplies could be expected. In their extremity Hudson Taylor and Mr. Jones contemplated selling some of their possessions. A Chinese merchant, when approached, expressed his willingness to buy a clock. But, alas! he demanded a week's trial of the timepiece ere he parted with his money. Quite natural, but... Their next expedient was to try to sell an old American stove to the foundry across the river. But again, alas! the bridge of boats had been carried away in the night by a flood, and their solitary cash would not pay the ferry. So the old stove had to be carried borne again! They were indeed brought into the net. But shut up unto God, He granted them a rich relief, compared with which the selling of the stove would have been a poor salvation.

"We went into the study and gave ourselves to waiting upon God," said Hudson Taylor. "We cried indeed unto the Lord in our trouble, and He heard and delivered us out of all our distresses. For while we were still upon our knees a letter arrived from England containing a remittance."

The letter conveyed a generous gift from Mr. Berger. Such a deliverance could not be suppressed. The whole story came out at the happy tea-party that evening! But while Hudson Taylor's heart was overflowing with joy at God's great goodness, he also recognized the serious aspect of such a situation, and told Maria Dyer that she must still regard herself as free if this should make her shrink from linking her lot with him.

"Have you forgotten," she quietly replied, "that I was left an orphan in a far-off land? God has been my Father all these years; and do you think that I shall be afraid to trust Him now?"

Could anything have more enhanced her value and increased his love? Here was a woman whose price was indeed above rubies. What music such words must have been to him as he listened! What a day to be remembered —God's deliverance, and such a woman's love! Is it to be wondered that Hudson Taylor said: "My heart did sing for joy." Such days are the alpine heights of the human heart.

Another fortnight, and January 20, the wedding day, dawned, and these two, already one in heart, solemnly plighted their troth to one another till death should them part. With an old Chinese temple to do duty for the Consulate, with Mr. Robert Hart, afterwards the famous Inspector-General of the Chinese Maritime Customs, as Acting Consul, and with the Rev. F. F. Gough, of the Church Missionary Society, as Chaplain, their vows were heard, and God's benediction besought.

Hudson Taylor wore his Chinese robes, and Maria Dyer a simple grey silk gown. The erstwhile almost "hopeless heights of hope were scaled, the summit won!" Sorrow was turned into joy, and for the spirit of heaviness they had received the garments of praise.

"Oh, to be married to the one you *do* love, and love most tenderly," Hudson Taylor wrote home some six weeks later. "This is bliss beyond the power of words to express or imagination to conceive. There is no disappointment there. And every day as it shows more of the mind of your Beloved, when you have such a treasure as mine, makes you only more proud, more happy, more humbly thankful to the Giver of all good for this best of all earthly gifts."

XII

GOD, THE ONE GREAT CIRCUMSTANCE

For nearly four years Hudson Taylor had been in China, and had suffered the lot of the pilgrim and the stranger. Like the Apostle Paul he had known what it was to be "buffeted"—not in body only—and to have "no certain dwelling-place." Now he was to enjoy that "most sweet and dear custom of living together" with the woman he loved. But that only made him feel the more that God must be his Eternal Home.

Those were days of constant peril and rude alarm. The mutiny in India had been a terrible demonstration of the dangers of life in the Far East. The Taiping Rebellion was a never-failing menace. Great Britain was still at war with China, and deeds of vengeance were ever possible. In Hongkong the chief baker had attempted to poison the foreign community. In Ningpo, where Hudson Taylor was, fifty or sixty Portuguese had been massacred in broad daylight, and had not the official— while the missionaries were actually at prayer—withdrawn his permission, a plot to murder all Europeans would probably have been successful. Such facts as these made "the secret place of the Most High" a great necessity and a glad reality. Hudson Taylor was learning to think of God as the One Great Circumstance in Whom he lived, and moved, and had his being.

For the first month or two of their married fife, after a brief sojourn in the quiet of a Chinese monastery, they made their home in a country district some ten miles from the city. But typhoid fever, which both contracted, drove them back to the city. Therefore, the Chinese house on Bridge Street, Ningpo, was remodelled and made a centre for settled work. And here the joys and anxieties of soul winning were experienced for the next eighteen months.

By day and by night these two were "in labours more abundant," dispensing to the sick, preaching to all who would listen, and teaching such as were interested. They had no efficient Chinese helpers, no attractive or expensive plant, only the devotion which was willing to spend and be spent for others. There was no withholding, no standing aloof from the people, always ready access and abounding sympathy, and that subtle power which touches souls and wins confidence. And the seed sown was well watered with their tears. There was a great expenditure of soul.

> "Perhaps," wrote Hudson Taylor, "if there were more of that intense distress for souls that leads to tears, we should more frequently see the results we desire." And again—and the following words throw light upon his methods—"How much of the precious time and strength of our Lord was spent in conferring temporal blessings on the poor, the afflicted and the needy. Such ministrations, proceeding from right motives, cannot be lost. They are Godlike, they are Christ like."

So by word, and by deed, they followed in the footsteps of Him who went about doing good. And the standard of discipleship was high. The keeping of the Sabbath, exacting as that was in China, was urged upon the little band of inquirers; and, that they might become a well-instructed company, a night school for learning to read the New Testament was instituted. For this work Hudson Taylor set great store, both then and subsequently, upon the Romanized version of the New Testament, as an aid to the illiterate.

Such labours were not in vain, for, within the space of twelve months from settling in at Bridge Street, there was established a little Church with eight members in communion. There was Tsiu the teacher and his mother; there was Fang the basket-maker, and Nyi the cotton merchant; there was

Wang the farmer, and Wang the painter; not to speak of others. For such a harvest in so short a time there was much cause for praise.

He was realizing God's presence and power to bless, and he was to prove God, in a time of acute crisis, as a Mighty One, able and willing to save.

It was Wednesday, February 9, 1859, a day long to be remembered, for Hudson Taylor stood, or kneeled, at the bedside of his dying wife. Every remedy seemed unavailing

> **SCRIPTURE TESTIMONY**
>
> *Don't be anxious, make requests known to God, and He will give peace*
>
> PHILIPPIANS 4:6-7

and all hope of recovery was almost gone. Life was fast ebbing away. Hudson Taylor had sent an urgent request for prayer to the missionary prayer meeting being held that afternoon, just then another remedy suggested itself to his mind, but he felt he must first consult Dr. Parker before using it, yet he was two miles away, and it seemed doubtful if his dear one's life could hold out till he returned.

> "It was a moment of anguish," he afterwards wrote. "The hollow temples, sunken eyes, and pinched features denoted the near approach of death; and it seemed more than questionable as to whether life would hold out until my return. It was nearly two miles to Dr. Parker's house, and every moment appeared long. On my way thither, while wrestling mightily with God in prayer, the precious words were brought with power to my soul: 'Call upon Me in the day of trouble; I will deliver thee, and thou shalt glorify Me.'"

The promise was pleaded in faith, and "a deep, deep, unspeakable peace and joy" filled his heart. All consciousness of distance was gone, though every moment before had seemed an age. It was the peace of God which passeth all understanding.

Dr. Parker, when consulted, approved the remedy suggested, but when Hudson Taylor reached home he found that the Great Physician Himself had been present and done His work. The pinched aspect of the countenance had given place to the calmness of tranquil slumber, and not one unfavourable symptom remained to retard full recovery. Such experiences of Divine intervention make the unseen real. Life can never again be quite the same. And Hudson Taylor and his wife both needed the abiding assurance of a God nigh at hand.

Owing to the kidnapping villainies of those engaged in the coolie traffic, public excitement not long after this reached a high pitch at Ningpo, and the lives and the property of the little European community were in imminent peril. Some of them indeed left the city, but Hudson Taylor and his wife would not forsake the little Christian community.

> "We are living," wrote Mr. Jones at this time, "from night to day and day to night. The people are thirsting for revenge. They mix up together missionaries, traders, and the government, the war, and the coolie traffic.... They have placarded the streets calling for our blood.... We are now in the midst of this, our wives and our little ones in the same danger. But we are resting on Him who restrains our enemies with 'thus far, but no further.'"

It was July, and the fierce heat of summer was almost insufferable, while the heat was aggravated by the angry crowds which surged without, and, at times, threatened to break in the doors. And that home on Bridge Street never stood in greater need of quiet and tranquillity. Yet the only precautions which could be taken, without actually leaving the premises, were a boat ready at the back door, and a rope in the bedroom window.

Amid such conditions, on Sunday, July 31, with the thermometer at 104° F. in the shade, their first-born child, a little girl, whom they named Grace, was welcomed to that storm-bound home. And the brave mother, with a heart stayed on God, and kept in perfect peace, made a good recovery. What lessons the very helplessness of that little babe must have taught them! "Can a woman forget her sucking child, that she should not have compassion on the son of her womb? Yea, they may forget, yet will I not forget thee." That mother in Ningpo could sing:

> "My child is lying on my knees;
> The signs of heaven she reads;
> My face is all the heaven she sees,
> Is all the heaven she needs.

"Lo! Lord I sit in Thy wide space,
My child upon my knee,
She looketh up unto my face,
And I look up to Thee."

But the angel of death was to visit that little company of brave souls in Ningpo, for before little Grace was a month old Dr. Parker was suddenly bereaved by the death of his wife and left with four motherless children. It was a shattering blow to him, and Dr. Parker felt compelled for the sake of his children, one of whom was seriously ill, as well as for his own health, to leave the work and return to Scotland.

It was a time of crisis for all, for Dr. Parker was the only medical man in Ningpo. Was the hospital with its fifty beds to close? And what about the dispensary? Dr. Parker urged Hudson Taylor to close the hospital but continue the dispensary. But this was to raise some big financial questions. Hitherto the expenses of that work had been met by the proceeds of Dr. Parker's European practice. This would now not be available, and the cost of upkeep and maintenance was considerable. Yet to close the hospital on these grounds alone would surely be a lack of faith in God.

> SCRIPTURE TESTIMONY
>
> *God's work will not lack God's supply*
>
> PHILIPPIANS 4:19
>
> *Ask Me anything in My name*
>
> MATTHEW 18:19 · JOHN 14:13-14 · JOHN 16:23-24
>
> *Seek first the Kingdom of God and His righteousness*
>
> MATTHEW 6:33

"Hath not God said," argued Hudson Taylor with himself, "that whatever we ask in the name of the Lord Jesus shall be done? And are we not told to seek first the Kingdom of God—not means to advance it—and that all these things shall be added to us? Such promises were surely sufficient."

To hold back on financial grounds, he felt, was nothing less than doubting God. And it was to fail God at a time of emergency. So he felt constrained to accept responsibility, not for the dispensary only, but also for the hospital. Eight days before he came to this decision he had not had the remotest idea of such a call, still less could his friends at home know. Yet funds were already on their way to meet this unknown and unexpected need! Is not our God the God of Abraham, who called the place of his trial *Jehovah Jireh?* "As it is said to this day, *In the Mount of the Lord it shall he provided.*"

How God would provide, Hudson Taylor did not know, but meanwhile he called together the hospital assistants and explained to them the situation, stating that he could not guarantee their salaries as Dr. Parker had, but that he would welcome their fellowship if they were prepared to trust God to supply their need, as he did. The fearful and the trembling departed, as they did from Gideon, and the remnant who remained were reinforced by some of the Bridge Street Christians. It was a new experience for all, and a trial of faith was to precede the glad experience of salvation.

The supplies in hand daily decreased, and at length, when the last bag of rice was reached, the wolf came to their very door. But prayer like incense was sent up

> "To God the strong, God the beneficent,
> God ever mindful in all strife and strait.
> Who, for our own good, makes the need extreme,
> Till at last He puts forth might and saves."

And then they saw God working for them, as they waited for Him. A letter arrived from Mr. Berger in England with a cheque for £50. But that was not all. The letter went on to state that the writer had recently lost his father, that he had inherited his property, that he did not purpose to increase his personal expenditure, could his friend in China tell him how some of this wealth could be used for God's glory? Truly "there is none like unto the Lord our God!"

After a season of thanksgiving with his wife, Hudson Taylor called the Chinese workers together and translated to them the letter. We can almost now hear their exclamations *Ai Ya?* What a lesson in faith, and in God's faithfulness! What a demonstration that the old message, "Fear not, stand still, and see the salvation of the Lord," is still applicable in the straits of human experience!

"I need not say," wrote Hudson Taylor, "how rejoiced they were, and that we praised God together. They returned to their work in the hospital with overflowing hearts, and told out to the patients what a God was ours, appealing to them whether their idols had ever helped them so. Both helpers and patients were spiritually blessed through this remarkable provision."

Other gifts followed, and not only were all financial needs supplied, but within nine months sixteen patients confessed their faith by baptism, while more than thirty others enrolled themselves as candidates.

But the burden of the work was too heavy for one man to carry alone, and the eyes of Hudson Taylor turned towards the home country for reinforcements. Writing to his parents in January, 1860, he said:

"Do you know any earnest, devoted young men desirous of serving God in China, who—not wishing for more than their actual support—would be willing to come out and labour here? Oh! for four or five such helpers! They would probably begin to preach in Chinese in six months, and in answer to prayer the necessary means for their support would be found."

Faith's capacity was being increased, and enlarged desires were beginning to possess his soul. Larger enterprises were suggesting themselves, and bolder expectations were coming to birth. But he was yet to know more fully the answer of death within himself that he might more absolutely set his hope on the God who raiseth the dead.

The incessant physical and mental strain entailed in the care of the hospital and other work had begun to imperil his own health, and even threatened life itself. He longed for the refreshment to be gained by a visit to the old country, but, with Dr. Parker away, how could he leave his post? He was in a strait betwixt two, having a desire for that rest and change which a visit home alone could afford, but, on the other hand, the hospital, and the little Church with its thirty to forty members, seemed to demand his presence. But at length complete prostration, consequent upon repeated attacks of illness and threatened tubercular trouble, made a visit to the more bracing climate of England the last and only hope of life.

With sad hearts the hospital was closed, and passages were booked for England. And so bountifully did God provide for the costly journey, that Hudson Taylor was able to take home, in addition to his wife and child, a Chinese Christian named Wang Lae-djun, to assist in literary work, and—yes, in faith—to instruct in the language those who might volunteer for the field.

It was in July, 1860, that the good ship *Jubilee,* in which they sailed, weighed anchor bound for London, nearly seven years having elapsed since Hudson Taylor had sailed from Liverpool. Then he had been but a youth of twenty-one, now he was a man of twenty- eight who had learned in the stem school of life to know God as his One Great Circumstance. And his love for China had deepened and increased by what he had seen of her vast and limitless need. "Had I a thousand pounds China should have it," he wrote his sister Amelia shortly before he left Shanghai. "Had I a thousand lives China should claim every one. No, not China, but Christ. Can we do too much for Him? Can we do enough for such a Saviour?" Such was the spirit in which he sailed for home.

XIII

A VISION SEEN THROUGH TEARS

IT IS easy now, in the light of after events, to see God's Hand in the sorrowful home-coming of Hudson Taylor; but then, to him, it was the deepest disappointment. It seemed the death-blow to many hopes, and nothing short of a great calamity. Nor was the sorrow lessened when, on reaching England, medical testimony assured him that all thought of returning to China for several years must be abandoned.

But God had said: "Light shall shine out of darkness," and faith still clung to God. Throughout the voyage earnest prayer was made that God would overrule, and turn this sorrow into joy, by making this time at home instrumental in the raising up of at least five helpers to labour in the province of Chekiang.

After a brief stay of a few months at Bayswater with Mr. and Mrs. Benjamin Broomhall, where their eldest son Herbert was born, Hudson Taylor and his wife rented a small house on a side street near the London Hospital in Whitechapel. Here, in scantily furnished rooms, he not only devoted himself to medical study, but also, in company with Rev. F. F. Gough of the Church Missionary Society, to the revision of the Ningpo New Testament. His medical degrees were secured in the late autumn of 1862, and then he was able to make the work upon the New Testament his chief occupation.

In this work of revision Hudson Taylor saw nothing beyond the use that the Book, with its marginal references, would be to the Chinese Christians, but in seeking to water others his own soul was watered and prepared for an unforeseen ministry. As he sat in his study, with the Scriptures on his desk, and a large map of China on the wall, there gradually dawned upon him, through his tears, a two-fold vision, in which God and China both had place. With the deeper sense of China's need came the fuller realization of Divine resources. The one was set over against the other. It was with him, as with Isaiah, "In the year that king Uzziah died I saw the Lord."

"While in the field," he wrote, "the pressure of claims immediately around me was so great that I could not think much of the still greater needs of the regions farther inland; and if they were thought of, could do nothing for them. But while detained for some years in England, daily viewing the whole country on the large map on the wall of my study, I was as near to the vast regions of Inland China as to the smaller districts in which I had laboured personally for God."

It is recorded of Napoleon, by his secretary, that when in Egypt, contemplating a march into India, "he spent whole days, lying flat on the ground stretched upon maps of Asia." What a contrast is that picture and this of Hudson Taylor in his humble home in London! What a different ambition stirred his heart as he surveyed the map of China! The cities, towns, and villages of that vast land were to him a field for service, not for self-aggrandizement. The countless millions without the Gospel moved him with compassion, as his Master had been moved by the hungry multitudes in the desert of Palestine. They must not be sent hungry away. But how could they be fed? Prayer was the only relief for his burdened heart, and this, with his daily study of God's Word, made him recognize the world's deepest need met by the fulness of God.

"I have often seen since," he wrote later, "that without those months of feeding and feasting on the Word of God, I should have been quite unprepared to form, on its present basis, a mission like the China Inland Mission.

"In the study of that Divine Word I learned that to obtain successful labourers, not elaborate appeals for help, but, *first*, earnest prayer to God to thrust forth labourers, and *second*, the deepening of the spiritual life of the Church, so that men should be unable to stay at home, were what was needed. I saw that the Apostolic plan was not to raise ways and means, but *to go and do the work*, trusting in His sure word who had said, 'seek ye *first* the Kingdom of God and His righteousness, and all these things shall be added unto you.'"

God's visions do not come to the idle dreamer, but to the man of toil, to Moses caring for the sheep, to Gideon and Oman threshing out the wheat, and to Matthew at the receipt of Custom. And so it was with Hudson Taylor. In the task of translation, with other duties, came that closer vision of God and the clearer sight of China's need.

What that vision of China was we know from *China's Spiritual Need and Claims,* a book published in the late autumn of 1865, but commenced long before, at the suggestion of the Rev. W. G. Lewis, Editor of the *Baptist Magazine.* It is a book which reminds us of Carey's *Enquiry,* save that Carey surveyed the world, while Hudson Taylor centres all his thought on China. If any refutation were ever needed that missionary enthusiasm sprang from an excess of emotion, such publications alone would provide a conclusive answer. In both cases history and facts are soberly marshalled to form an irresistible argument. Carey's keynote is "obligation." It occurs in his title: *An Enquiry into the Obligations of Christians.* And Hudson Taylor's key-thought was *need and claims,* with the terrible reminder *"If thou forbear."* If, as Milton says, "A good book is the precious lifeblood of a master spirit," that was eminently true in this case. The facts and statistics throb with life and pulsate with deep feeling. The book was a *cri de cœur.*

China's Spiritual Need and Claims is a small book of about one hundred and twenty pages, and opens with the words:

"If thou forbear to deliver them that are drawn unto death, and those that are ready to be slain;

"If thou sayest, Behold, we knew it not; doth not He that pondereth the heart consider it? and He that keepeth thy soul, doth not He know it? and shall not He render to every man according to his works?"

This verse is repeated like a refrain time and again throughout the little volume, for the facts are arrayed so as to convict the reader of his and her responsibility. What the writer asked for was, "not vain words of empty sympathy, but effectual, fervent prayer, and strenuous self-denying effort"

After a brief introduction referring to the momentous consequences of our every thought and every act, he asks the reader to reflect on the great antiquity, the vast extent, the teeming population of China, its spiritual destitution, and its overwhelming need. When these themes have been considered with impressive detail, there follows a brief survey of what has been done for China's good, and then the reader is asked to contemplate the work that still remains.

First the seven maritime provinces (including Hupeh on the Yangtse) in which Protestant missionaries were labouring, are studied, and it is shown that, if each missionary had a parish equal to eight of our principal English cities, there would still be 185 millions of people for whom no provision had been made. And further, this deplorable fact emerges in the study, viz. that the total number of Protestant missionaries in China had actually fallen off from 115 in 1860, to 90 or 91 in March, 1865. Yet he adds, "since the last Treaty with China, more Romish missionaries and sisters of charity have gone thither than the whole staff of Protestant missionaries." And grievous as these facts were, he proceeded to show that the state of the rest of the empire was even more distressing.

It is the cumulative effect of the facts solemnly arrayed that impresses the reader, but space will not permit us to do more than summarize his statements. Of the eleven inland, and totally unoccupied provinces, the following is the briefest précis:

> Kansu,[1] larger than France and Spain together, had no missionary.
> Szechwan, nearly as large as Sweden, had no missionary.

---

1   This province then included most of Sinkiang.

Yunnan, as large as Prussia, had no missionary.

Shensi, equal in extent to Holland, Saxony, Bavaria, and Wurtemberg, had no missionary.

Shansi, nearly as large as England and Wales, had no missionary.

Honan, as large as the Austrian States, had no missionary.

Anhwei, a little smaller than England, had no missionary.

Kiangsi, twice the size of Portugal, had no missionary.

Hunan, nearly one-third larger than Austria, had no missionary.

Kweichow, larger than Belgium, Saxony, Hanover, and Bavaria, had no missionary.

Kwangsi, nearly equal in extent to England and Wales, had no missionary.

Here were eleven provinces, with a total population of 1974 millions, for whose good not a single Protestant missionary was labouring. Add to these the neglected 185 millions of the other provinces, and you have a total exceeding 380 millions absolutely without those tidings which the Saviour long ago commanded to be carried to every creature. And in addition, there were the outlying dependencies of Manchuria, Mongolia, Ili, Tsinghai, and Tibet.

"We fear," wrote Hudson Taylor, "lest our readers should weary of these details; but though they may seem uninteresting, they are important and solemn realities. Whether interesting to us or not, every individual of the millions of China, every inhabitant of these vast regions, must either live for ever or die for ever.... Every day 33,000, every month 1,000,000 subjects of the Chinese Emperor pass into eternity, without ever having heard the Gospel; and though we may say, 'Behold, we knew it not,' God will not justify our leaving them to perish on the ground of that excuse."

He then proceeded to show the feasibility of a more extensive evangelization of China. Treaty provisions were quoted, and some impressive experiences of God's providential interpositions on his behalf were related. It might seem to some a hazardous experiment to send out workers to China with God only to look to, but to one who had proved God at home and abroad, by land and by sea, in sickness and health, in necessity, in danger, and at the gates of death, such apprehension seemed inexcusable.

"The writer," Hudson Taylor continued, "has seen God, in answer to prayer, quell the raging of the storm, alter the direction of the wind, and give rain in the midst of a prolonged drought. He has seen Him, in answer to prayer, stay the angry passions and murderous intentions of violent men, and bring the machinations of His people's foes to nought. He has seen Him, in answer to prayer, raise the dying from the bed of death, when human aid was vain; has seen Him preserve from the pestilence that walketh in darkness, and from the destruction that wasteth at noonday. For more than eight and a half years he has proved the faithfulness of God in supplying the pecuniary means for his temporal wants, and for the needs of the work he has been engaged

"Shall not the eternal interests of one-third of our race stir the deepest sympathies of our nature, the most strenuous efforts of our blood-bought powers? Shall not the low wail of helpless, hopeless misery, arising from half the heathen world, pierce our sluggish ears, and rouse us—body, soul, and spirit—to one mighty, continued, unconquerable effort for China's weal."

"It is the prayerful consideration of these facts, and the deepening realization of China's awful destitution of all that can make man truly happy, that constrain the writer, by every means in his power, to lay its claims as a heavy burden upon the hearts of those who have already experienced the power of the blood of Christ."

These few extracts will give the reader some conception of the facts which had burned themselves into the mind and heart of the writer. They were before him day and night, and every glance at that map on the wall brought these great realities home to his heart afresh. There was no escape from them, they were facts stamped upon his mind by what he had seen in China itself. They were to him the burden of the Lord. "If thou forbear to deliver them.... He that keepeth thy soul, doth not He know it? and shall not He render to every man according to his works?" To a man who implicitly believed God's Word to be true, the solemn bearing of every act and every omission on the future welfare of God's children, and on that of others, was inescapable.

But we have only considered one of the two visions which were ever before his eyes. We have contemplated briefly his view of the need; there was also the vision of God, and of His unsearchable supplies. There was not only the map with its story of human woe, there was the Bible with its revelation of God Himself, and of His boundless mercy and faithfulness. It must be remembered that Hudson Taylor was detained in England for nearly five and a half years, and that for the greater part of this time he was daily engaged in the revision of the Ningpo version of the New Testament. After the completion of his medical studies, he had frequently devoted himself to this work of New Testament revision from eight to twelve hours a day, and sometimes more. Any student will recognize, what concentration of thought this means. It is more than many strong men could endure, and it speaks eloquently for Hudson Taylor's mental powers and passionate devotion.

And again, is there any other pursuit which can so impress a man with the value and significance of words. Bishop Westcott, one of the greatest of New Testament scholars, has said: "If I am to select one endowment which I have found precious for the whole work of life beyond all others, it would be the belief in words which I gained through the severest discipline of verbal criticism. Belief in words is the foundation of belief in thought, and of belief in man." He might have added, "and of belief in God."

Hudson Taylor had proved God in China, and he had proved God in East London, for some of his acutest tests of faith in matters of finance came while he was there. Time and again deliverance came at the eleventh hour, and sometimes later. Rent and taxes had been due when funds were insufficient, but only once was payment deferred, and then for less than forty-eight hours. These experiences only served to emphasize God's faithfulness, and the open Bible made him dwell deep in God's truth. God was taking a larger and larger place in his life and outlook. More and more he was conscious that he lived, and moved, and had his being in God, that if God were with him, and for him, it did not matter who, or what, was against him.

While on the one hand he saw the great and solemn responsibilities, on the other he saw "the gracious encouragements that everywhere meet us in God's Word."

> "The Word had said: 'seek first the Kingdom of God and His righteousness, and all these things (food and raiment) shall be added unto you.' If anyone did not believe that God spoke the truth, it would be better for him not to go to China to propagate the faith. If he did believe it, surely the promise sufficed. Again, 'No good thing will He withhold from them that walk uprightly.' If anyone did not mean to walk uprightly he had better stay at home. If he did mean to walk uprightly, he had all he needed in the shape of a guarantee fund. God owns all the silver and the gold in the world, and the cattle on a thousand hills. We need not be vegetarians!"

He believed in God, and he implicitly believed in God's Word. He was prepared to step out upon it, to venture all upon its veracity, to risk life, and all that life holds dear, in the faith that heaven and earth shall pass away, but God's Word shall abide, that "the Word of our God shall stand for ever." God to him was real, His Word was real, and the needs of the world were real. He was living in the realm of reality. God was nigh, "ever intimately near." As one of our poet sages has written:

> "To make things real to us is the end and the battle- cause of life. We often think we believe what we are only presenting to our imaginations. The least thing can overthrow that kind of faith. The imagination is an endless help towards faith, but it is no more faith than a dream of food will make us strong for the next day's work. To know God, as the beginning and the end, the root and cause, the giver, the enabler, the love and joy and perfect good, the present One existence in all things and degrees and conditions, is life; and faith in its truest, mightiest form is—to do His Will."

Hudson Taylor would have nothing to do with Mr. Clip-Promise who sought to debase the King's coin. The Word of God was to him the Coin of God's realm, and it was not going to be less than a Bank of England note.

"The living God still lives," he wrote, "and the living Word is a living word, and we may depend upon it; we may hang upon any word that God ever spoke, or ever caused by His Holy Spirit to be written....

"If the Bible were not true, the sooner we found it out and threw it aside the better; but if it is true, the sooner we live up to it and act up to it the better. If any of you were offered a Bank of England note, whether for five pounds or five thousand pounds, you would never doubt the value of it. You would take the words printed on it as sure. And are not the words printed in this Book as sure? No part of the Book is unworthy of our credit. It is either God's word, or it is not what it is represented to be."

God was his Father, and prayer to him was "a word to the Big Heart from the little one." One of his many proverbial utterances was: "Before I was a father I thought God never would forget me; but since I have been a father I know God never can forget me." It was the application of Christ's words: "If ye then, being evil, know how to give good gifts unto your children, how much more shall your Heavenly Father?"

"Our Father is a very experienced One," he once wrote. "He knows very well that His children wake up

SCRIPTURE TESTIMONY
God's work will not lack God's supply
PHILIPPIANS 4:19

with a good appetite every morning, and He always provides breakfast for them, and does not send them supperless to bed at night. 'Thy bread shall be given thee, and thy water shall be sure.' He sustained three million Israelites in the wilderness for forty years. We do not expect He will send three million missionaries to China, but if He did, He would have ample means to sustain them all. Let us see that we keep God before our eyes; that we walk in His ways and seek to please and glorify Him in everything, great and small. Depend upon it, God's work done in God's way will never lack God's supplies."

God was becoming all in all to him. God was not a God afar off, but nigh at hand. God was his Father and he His child, and the childlike spirit became his strength. "Have faith in God" meant more and more as years rolled by. He learned to "lean more constantly, to draw more largely, to rest more implicitly, on the strength, the riches, and the fulness" of God in Christ. And one verse which he frequently inscribed in people's birthday books, or autograph albums, was: "The Lord thy God is in the midst of thee, a Mighty One who will save; He will rejoice over thee with joy, He will rest in His love, He will joy over thee with singing." And the joy of the Lord became his strength.

PART III

1865-1905
THE MISSIONARY LEADER
AET. 33-73

HE GAVE SOME TO BE APOSTLES
AND SOME PROPHETS
AND SOME EVANGELISTS
AND SOME PASTORS AND TEACHERS
FOR THE PERFECTING OF THE SAINTS
UNTO THE WORK OF MINISTERING
UNTO THE BUILDING UP OF THE BODY OF CHRIST

Ephesians 4:11, 12

XIV

"THOU HAST PREVAILED"

ETWEEN THE writing of the first and last pages of *China's Spiritual Need and Claims* the best part of a year elapsed. At the request of the Rev. W. G. Lewis, Hudson Taylor had, early in 1865, commenced a series of articles for publication in *The Baptist Magazine*, but Mr. Lewis, after printing the first of these, recognized that what was being written deserved a wider public than he could command. He therefore suggested that the articles be enlarged to cover the whole of Inland China, and that they be published separately. This entailed further study and prayer, and the manuscript, in its final form, was not completed before the middle of October. Meanwhile, Hudson Taylor had faced one of the most momentous crises of his life, the decisive moment which gave birth to the China Inland Mission.

This crisis was the inevitable result of the vision seen through tears. As he meditated on the book, and paced his room dictating its pages to his wife, he felt "God's sigh in the heart of the world." As he mused the fire burned. The sense of China's need grew and over-whelmed him; and at the same time a consciousness of God's willingness to do greater things possessed his soul. He had come home from China prepared to ask for five devoted workers, and God was giving these. But the inadequacy of so small a number became more evident, as the urgency and magnitude of the need dominated his mind.

Day by day it became increasingly clear that God was speaking. The Revival, then in progress, was a revelation in the home-land of God's power to bless, while a million a month dying in China without God was its appalling contrast. The larger missionary societies, which had been approached, had professed themselves unable to undertake greater responsibilities, and the unsuccessful efforts made in this direction gave rise to a deep conviction that a special agency was needed for the evangelization of inland China. He felt assured that, in answer to prayer, workers would be given, and their support provided, for he knew that nothing was too hard for God. But he shrank from the conclusion, which was being forced upon him, that God wanted *him* to ask for these workers, and to go forth with them as their leader. Thus was he brought into the Valley of Decision.

Vision and decision are never far apart, as all God's prophets have experienced. And all pleaded their insufficiency, for obedience to the heavenly vision was never lightly undertaken. This was not rebellion, but the soul staggered by a new and great responsibility, before it had grasped afresh the truth that God was greater still. It was the swift and overwhelming appreciation of the magnitude of the command, and the more tardy recovery of faith recognizing that "the King's word hath power."[1]

Some such exercise of soul seems almost inevitable with finite man. It is the process by which he learns to cast himself more fully upon God. It is the soul regaining its poise as it advances one foot at a time. The cry, "Who is sufficient for these things?" precedes the confidence, "Our sufficiency is of God." The one leads to the other, where faith is. And so, God who calls confirms. To this end He told Moses His Name: I AM THAT I AM. And the Lord looked upon Gideon, and said: "Go in this thy might... have not I sent thee?" Again, one of the seraphim touched the lips of Isaiah with a live coal from off the altar; and the Lord said to Jeremiah: "Say not, I am a child... for I am with thee."

---

1   Compare the experience and testimony of Martin Luther: "From the bottom of my soul, I call God to witness, that I should have continued in my fear, should have hesitated and hesitated up to the present day, and onward, had not my conscience, had not the force of truth compelled me to speak. I fought with myself, till Jesus Christ, by His own infallible Word, fortified my heart against these doubts, till it became as a coast of rocks, defying the waves which impotently dash against it."

Hudson Taylor was treading the same path. He had learned to trust God for himself; but to trust God for others was a larger and more exacting undertaking.

"I had no doubt," he wrote, "that, if I prayed for workers in the Name of the Lord Jesus Christ, they would be given me. I had no doubt that, in answer to such prayer, the means for our going forth would be

SCRIPTURE TESTIMONY
The weary are invited to receive rest from Jesus
MATTHEW 11:28-29
Don't be anxious, make requests known to God, and He will give peace
PHILIPPIANS 4:6-7

provided, and that doors would be opened before us in unreached parts of the Empire. But I had not then learned to trust God for keeping power and grace for myself, so no wonder that I could not trust Him to keep others who might be prepared to go with me.

"I feared that in the midst of the dangers, difficulties, and trials which would necessarily be connected with such a work [and he knew how great these were], some who were comparatively inexperienced Christians might break down, and bitterly reproach me for having encouraged them to undertake such an enterprise for which they were unequal.

"Yet, what was I to do? The feeling of blood-guiltiness became more and more intense. Simply because I refused to ask for them, the labourers did not come forward—did not go out to China—and every day tens of thousands were passing away into Christless graves! Perishing China so filled my heart and mind that there was no rest by day, and little sleep by night, till health broke down."

The words so often quoted in his little book rang continually in his ears: "If thou forbear to deliver them that are drawn unto death, and those that are ready to perish; ...doth not He that pondereth the heart consider it? and He that keepeth thy soul, doth not He know it?" And Jeremiah's experience was repeated, when he wrote: "If I say, I will not make mention of Him, nor speak any more in His Name, then there is in my heart as it were a burning fire shut up in my bones, and I am weary of forbearing, and I cannot contain." Hudson Taylor was face to face with One who was stronger than he.

> "For two or three months," he wrote, "the conflict was intense. I scarcely slept night or day more than an hour at a time, and feared I should lose my reason. Yet I did not give in. To no one could I speak freely, not even to my dear wife. She doubtless saw that something was going on, but I felt I must refrain as long as possible from laying upon her a burden so crushing—these souls, and what eternity must mean for every one of them, and what the Gospel might do, would do, for all who believed, if we would take it to them."

It was impossible a conflict so intense should last indefinitely. The day of the Lord was near in the Valley of Decision. His honoured friend, Mr. George Pearse, concerned at his state of health, but not divining the cause, invited Hudson Taylor to spend a few days with him at Brighton, and to this invitation he responded. And it was there upon the sands of the seashore—the sands which recall the promises and blessings of God to Abraham of old—that another man, being tried, offered up himself. The story must be told in his own words:

> "On Sunday, June 25th, 1865, unable to bear the sight of a congregation of a thousand or more Christian people rejoicing in their own security, while millions were perishing for lack of knowledge, I wandered out on the sands alone, in great spiritual agony; and there the Lord conquered my unbelief, and I surrendered myself for this service. I told Him that all the responsibility as to issues and consequences must rest with Him, that as His servant, it was mine to obey and follow Him—His, to direct, to care for, and to guide me and those who might labour with me."

Henceforth it was to be an absolute and unreserved obedience to the all-conquering Lord. Like Jeremiah he could say: "O Lord, Thou hast enticed me, and I was enticed; Thou art stronger than I, and hast prevailed."

And, like Jeremiah, he was to issue forth from this struggle more sure of God, more trustful in Him, and also able to say: "The Lord is with me as a Mighty One.... Blessed is the man that trusteth in the Lord, and whose hope the Lord is. For he shall be as a tree planted by the waters, and that spreadeth out her roots by the river, and shall not see when heat cometh, but her leaf shall be green; and shall not be careful in the year of drought, neither shall cease from yielding fruit." He had added courage to his faith, and henceforth was to have "that power of conviction which doubles the strength of the strong."

His Bible was in his hand, and his portion for that day, as his dated Bible shows, was in the Book of Job where it reads:

> "Oh that my words were now written!
> Oh that they were inscribed in a book!
> That with an iron pen and lead
> They were graven in the rock for ever!"

And so, as he prayed for twenty-four fellow-workers, two for each of the eleven inland provinces which were without a missionary, and two for Mongolia, he wrote upon the margin of his Bible, while peace flowed into his burdened heart:

> *Prayed for twenty-four willing, skilful labourers at Brighton June 25, 1865.*

And that Bible, with this historic record, and a pencil mark against the passage quoted above, still remains a treasured memorial of that memorable occasion.

"How restfully I turned from the shore when this was done," wrote Hudson Taylor. "The conflict was all ended. Peace and gladness filled my soul. I felt almost like flying up that steep hill by the station to Mr. Pearse's house, and how I did sleep that night! My dear wife thought that Brighton had done wonders for me; and so it had!"

XV

THE MEEK INHERIT

THE GREAT transaction at Brighton, which was both a prayer and a consecration, was sealed two days later by the opening, in the London and County Bank, of an account in the name of the China Inland Mission, with the sum of £10. Both the name and the amount are arresting, for it is the first time the name appears, and the sum seems small indeed with which to start a Mission to evangelize inland China! But it was £10, "and all the promises of God," as Hudson Taylor said on a subsequent occasion. It was faith's mustard seed, and since that date approximately four million pounds sterling have been paid in to the Bank on account of the same Mission. "It is all the same to God whether we begin with ten pounds or a thousand," said an old Scotch saint, who probably never heard of Hudson Taylor, but believed in the same Heavenly Father.

From this time onward there appears a new note, or more correctly a new tone in Hudson Taylor's life. The note or theme was still the evangelization of China, but a stronger confidence, and a more joyful assurance run like a deep diapason through everything. "I much need to add to faith courage," he wrote to his wife not long after the Brighton experience.[1] And this he did. He did not court publicity, but the day for it had come. The years of

---

1   Is it possible he had in mind the exhortation of Peter, "Add to your faith virtue," the Greek arete, primarily meaning courage, resolution, prowess?

obscure labour were past, there was now to be recognition and leadership. What he had learned in the checkered months and lowly spheres at Shanghai, Swatow, Ningpo, and East London was now to be employed in a larger service. Those hidden years had been God's preparation. They were his apprenticeship in missionary methods, when principles were proved, plans laid, and practical experience gained. He was now, though only thirty-three, well versed in the use of the Christian's spiritual weapons. "The signs of an apostle" had been wrought in him, in all patience. As the great Apostle of the Gentiles had for fourteen years served first as an obscure pioneer, and then as a junior colleague to Barnabas, before he entered into the full tide of his activities, so Hudson Taylor had laboured for twelve years in silence, and patience, in a narrow and humble sphere, and had become thereby versed in the ways of God. He had proved himself faithful "over a few things;" he was now to be set "over many things."

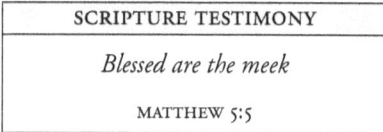

SCRIPTURE TESTIMONY

Blessed are the meek

MATTHEW 5:5

"Blessed are the meek, for they shall inherit the earth," said our Saviour, and Hudson Taylor's life was to exemplify the truth of these words. Notable friendships now came to him, men and women were attracted to him as leader, funds were entrusted to him, closed provinces were opened before him, and stations occupied for the preaching of the Gospel. The meek do not possess by force, but, as children, by inheritance. And the childlike spirit was Hudson Taylor's strength and secret.

We do not purpose telling in any detail the story of the China Inland Mission—that has been done elsewhere. The object of this book is to study Hudson Taylor himself, yet obviously the man cannot be separated wholly from his work. Six workers had sailed for China prior to that memorable Sunday at Brighton, two more were to follow shortly, and Hudson Taylor with his wife, four children, and sixteen workers (ten women and six men) were to follow in May, 1866, in the *Lammermuir*.

The eleven months which were to elapse between Brighton and the sailing of this large party were crowded with fruitful and far-reaching service. With his heart now at liberty to express itself without reserve he completed his little book *China's Spiritual Need and Claims,* every sentence being literally steeped in prayer. And other means for reaching God's people were used. The Annual Conference at Perth—the Keswick of those days—was attended, and an opportunity obtained, with some difficulty, to speak on the missionary question. At the Mildmay Conference in October he also spoke, and with the Rev. W. Pennefather's sympathetic approval his little book, just ready in time, was distributed to many hundreds of interested friends. And the influence of that little volume was both immediate and lasting. Many hearts were deeply impressed, and a second edition was called for in the course of a few weeks. Further editions and reprints followed over a course of many years. Even in the 'eighties, an edition was exhausted in four months, and two more reprints followed almost immediately. Its burning message, born in his heart, spoke to the heart, and bore fruit for eternity.

The authentic note is generally recognized. It was so now, and loyal friends began to multiply. During the next few months a strong bond of practical sympathy was established between himself and George Müller, Robert Chapman, Lord Radstock, Lady Beauchamp and family, Henry Bewley, William Fry, Mr. Grattan Guinness, and many others. Candidates, too, began to offer, attracted by his zeal, and his call for the heroic in the cause of Christ, one of these being Thomas Barnardo, who, while studying medicine with a view to China, felt the stronger call of London's children. Over £900 was received in the latter half of 1865, and, as more candidates volunteered, larger sums were given, and larger premises were secured in Coborn Road for the growing numbers. And, as December closed, the last day of the old year was set aside for waiting upon God in prayer and fasting, a custom then established and maintained ever since.

The new year was entered upon with fresh assurance, bolder resolution, and larger enterprises. The first official organ of the Mission was launched under the title of *Occa-*

> SCRIPTURE TESTIMONY
>
> *God answers prayer*
>
> LUKE 18:7 · JOHN 15:7 ·
> ACTS 12:5 · JAMES 5:15

sional Papers. On February 6, the manuscript of the first number was sent to the printer, with a statement that a sum of £1500 to £2000 would be required for a party which would D.V. sail in May. Owing to delays, occasioned in the engraving of the cover and a fire at the printer's, this number was not ready for publication until March 12, by which time £1974 had been received in answer to prayer alone. It therefore became necessary to use a coloured inset to inform the readers that the sum mentioned had already been met. "Truly," wrote Hudson Taylor, "there is a *living God,* and He is the Hearer and Answerer of prayer."

Other striking tokens of God's gracious provision followed. The Chairman at one meeting urged Hudson Taylor to consent to a collection, but, as one of his principles was no soliciting of funds, he courteously declined. The result was that the Chairman, who was also Hudson Taylor's host, told him next morning that while he had purposed giving £5, during the night he had been so exercised that he felt compelled to give £500, which sum he there and then handed to Mr. Taylor. The same morning Hudson Taylor had received the offer of the whole of the accommodation of the *Lammermuir.* The ship was found suitable, Colonel Puget's cheque was paid down on account, the simultaneous offer of this vessel's accommodation and this munificent gift being accepted as God's ratification of this great venture of faith.

It is interesting to note, at this time, the appearance of a new watchword. The two mottoes *Jehovah-Jireh* and *Ebenezer* had been adopted long before in China. Now to these was added a third, *Jehovah-Nissi,* "The Lord my Banner." It is first seen on the cover of *Occasional Papers,* and well suits the thought of a forward movement, of an aggressive adventure with the Lord Himself as Captain of the host. It serves, too, to show how God was in all his thoughts; it was God who had delivered, it was God who would provide, and it was God who must direct every step of the way.

The secret of Hudson Taylor's strength was God. As the Russians are said to have a standard word for "The Godseeker," so we seem to need a word to indicate the God-conscious devotee, the man who is always aware of God, who lives as seeing Him Who is invisible. This was Hudson Taylor's attitude. With the Psalmist he could say:

> "I have set the Lord always before me.
> Because He is at my right hand, I shall not be moved."

This was the key of his life. This was the potent truth which made him what he was. All his guiding principles he culled from God's Word. He dared to put Christ's precepts into practice. He dared to "resist not evil," to turn the other cheek, to seek first God's kingdom, and trust for the rest. Difficulties did not daunt him, but only made him the more resolute.

"Every difficulty overcome by faith," he said, "is 'bread'—strength and nourishment—to the child of God. Such the Anakims might have proved to Israel, but Israel failed, and we too often fail from want of faith."

In this way he made his antagonist his helper. The spirit in which he went forth, and the spirit in which he builded, is perhaps best illustrated by some extracts from a paper he wrote not long afterwards as a guide to would-be candidates. It shows how deeply he had meditated on the mind of Christ, and how he sought to win by faith, by love, by patience, and by meekness.

"Had our Lord appeared on earth as an angel of light, He would doubtless have inspired far more awe and reverence, and would have collected together even larger multitudes to attend His ministry. But to save man He became man, not merely like man, but very man.... In language, in costume, in everything unsinful, He made Himself one with those He sought to benefit.

"Had He been born a noble Roman, rather than a Jew, He would, perhaps, if less loved, have commanded more of a certain kind of

> SCRIPTURE TESTIMONY
>
> *Become all things to all people*
>
> I CORINTHIANS 9:19-23

respect; and He would assuredly thereby have been spared much indignity to which He was subjected. This, however, was not His aim; He emptied Himself. Surely no follower of the meek and lowly Jesus will be likely to conclude that it is 'beneath the dignity of a Christian missionary' to seek identification with this poor people, in the hope that he may see them washed, sanctified, and justified in the name of the Lord Jesus, and by the Spirit of our God!...

"I am not peculiar in holding the opinion that the foreign dress and carriage of missionaries—to a certain extent affected by some of their converts and pupils—the foreign appearance of the chapels, and, indeed, the foreign air given to everything connected with religion, have very largely hindered the rapid dissemination of the truth among the Chinese. But why should such a foreign aspect be given to Christianity? The Word of God does not require it; nor, I conceive, could sound reason justify it."

In the light of recent developments in China how sane all this appears. What troubles might have been avoided if all had seen and felt like this!

"Let us," he continues, "in everything not sinful, become Chinese, that by all means we may save some. Let us adopt their costume, acquire their language, study to imitate their habits, and approximate to their diet as far as health and constitution will allow. Let us live in their houses, making no unnecessary alterations in external form, and only as far modifying their internal arrangements as attention to health and efficiency for work absolutely require....

"This cannot, of course, be attained without some measure of inconvenience.... But will anyone reflect on what He gave up who left heaven's throne to be cradled in a manger... who being the Loved One of the Father, never unappreciated, never misunderstood, and receiving the ceaseless adoration of the hierarchies of heaven, became a despised Nazarene, misunderstood by His most faithful fol-lowers, suspected by those who owed to Him their very being, and whose salvation He had come to seek; and finally, mocked, and spit upon, crucified and slain, with thieves, bandits, and outlaws. Will, I ask, any brother or sister reflect on this, and yet hesitate to make the trifling sacrifice to which we have alluded?...

"But, once let the question arise, 'Are we called to give up this, or that, or the other?' or admit the thought, 'I did not expect this or that privation or inconvenience,' and your service will cease to be that free and happy one which is most conducive to efficiency and success. 'God loveth a cheerful giver.'"

There is much more in the same spirit, but this must suffice to show how truly he had apprehended the mind of his Master, and to indicate the spirit he sought to infuse in those who wished to follow him. That he was not asking what he did not practise himself all knew, and that added power to his words. His strength as a leader lay in his example, even more than in his precept. No trial was shirked, no sacrifice considered too great. He knew soul travail, depths of feeling, he knew something of the griefs and joys of the Christian worker, and the expenditure of soul and heart in his work. And his spirit was contagious, and multiplied itself. He could attach people both to himself and to his principles, and this was in no small measure because of his own large heart and his humble, human sympathies. The meek inherited.

XVI

THE AUDACITY OF FAITH

O N SATURDAY, May 26, 1866, Hudson Taylor, his wife and four children, together with one married couple, five single men, and nine unmarried

SCRIPTURE TESTIMONY
Take the gospel to the ends of the earth
MARK 16:15 · ACTS 1:8 · ACTS 6:7 · COLOSSIANS 1:23

women, a party of twenty-two in all, set sail for China in the *Lammermuir*, a three-masted sailing ship of 760 tons burden. To all but Mr. and Mrs. Hudson Taylor, the Land of Sinim was an unknown country. They were going out, not knowing whither they went. They had no one at home to guarantee them support; they had no one in China to welcome them; they had no home ready to receive them; there were no unmarried European women anywhere in China away from the ports; and yet there were nine unmarried women in the party, and all were destined to the interior of an anti-foreign country. It was a daring adventure, without precedent, and certain of criticism.

To many such audacity was unwise, to others it was presumption, and to some, especially in Shanghai, reckless folly, and calling for official intervention. But in Hudson Taylor burned the flame of a passionate belief, and from such master-passions come "the great miracles of action in history." He knew his God, was strong, and did exploits. He believed, to quote his own words, "in the wisdom, as well as the blessedness, of literally obeying the Scriptures," and was prepared to stake his all upon them. He was assured that "the eyes of the Lord run to and fro throughout the whole earth, to show Himself strong on behalf of those whose hearts are perfect toward Him." And so, like the old Breton fishermen, when they launched their slender craft upon the mighty Atlantic, he could pray in confidence: "O my God, succour me, my bark is so small, and Thy sea is so great." It was indeed a great sea out into which that little company launched, and to anyone who will pause to consider the possibilities of disaster the audacity of faith becomes an awe-inspiring fact.

SCRIPTURE TESTIMONY

Believers are the aroma of Christ to those around them

2 CORINTHIANS 2:14-16

Christians care for one another in love

JOHN 13:34-35 · I JOHN 3:11-24

And the perils were not all external. It needs but a little acquaintance with human nature to know that the dangers of dissolution come more frequently from within than from without. The *Lammermuir* party was composed of men and women drawn from all classes, and endowed with divergent natures. Some came from refined homes, others from less cultured circles, and for such a company to be shut up within the limits of a small ship, for four months at sea, away from their normal avocations, made demands on grace, and on the wisdom of their leader, of a highly practical nature. The spiritual usefulness of the little Mission could have been stifled at its birth had Hudson Taylor been other than he was. That he was able, from the first, to imbue all these varied elements with his own devotion, to inspire them by his example, to maintain their passion for souls, to overcome friction when it arose, and to create, by his own loving headship, a family feeling among persons of such varied temperaments is one of the greatest tributes to his God-given powers. Before Shanghai was reached more than twenty out of a crew of thirty-four had confessed their faith in Christ, a fact which bears its own witness to the life of the missionary band on board. "Crossing the sea never made a missionary" was an oft repeated phrase of Hudson Taylor's, for he had small faith in the usefulness of those who expected to be abroad what they were not at home. The two terrible typhoons, which dismasted and almost sank the vessel ere she reached her destination, though more spectacular, were not as deadly a peril as that which had been conquered within the cabins of that ship. Though the Mission has stood in jeopardy every hour of its history, this jeopardy stands out with a dramatic vividness as we picture the newly born organization shut up for so long within the limits of that little vessel, in the midst of the perils of the mighty deep.

Shanghai was reached on Sunday morning, the last day of September, 1866. That the vessel was in a badly battered and dismantled state only served to remind its passengers that even the winds and waves are subject to their Master's word. They had learned that Christ had been with them in the storm, and were strengthened for trials ahead.

Terrible as the unfriendly forces of Nature are, the opposition of man can be even more disconcerting. And so Shanghai, though a welcome refuge from the storms at sea, was a somewhat inhospitable haven for such an unconventional missionary party. Here the cutting criticism of the unsympathetic had to be faced, and the difficulty of securing accommodation for so large a party, for Shanghai was small in those days. And then the more serious problem of taking such a company of raw recruits inland, and of finding for them some place of residence in the heart of an anti-foreign city—when it was frequently impossible to gain a footing for one— had to be undertaken. This was enough to make most men quail, but he who believed that the walls of Jericho fell down by faith knew that to occupy China's fenced cities also was not impossible with God. And he was not confounded, for in Shanghai a Mr. Gamble lent his go-down, and at Hangchow—all other cities en route having closed their gates—a Mr. Kreyer lent his house during a week's absence. And improbable, and impossible, as it humanly appeared, Chinese premises were secured just before this kind friend returned with wife and child. There was no margin of time to spare, but "God's clocks keep good time," as Hudson Taylor said, and the timely help was given.

But formidable as the difficulties were, and strong as was the faith that faced them, Hudson Taylor was of no stem and ascetic build. He had always the saving grace of humour. Weighty responsibilities, and awkward situations, did not overwhelm him or make him harsh, for he possessed in large measure the power to see the ludicrous and mirthful aspect of most questions. It is doubtful if sufficient emphasis has been laid upon this side of his character, which was perhaps more seen in the playful smile which lit up his conversation than appears in his writings. Yet they appear there also. Take, for instance, the following description of the Mission's first premises at Lanchi, whither Duncan went as pioneer:

> "I left Duncan in what we consider comfortable lodgings for travellers, a roof over his head, more or less leaky, of course, but still a roof; a floor under his feet, and not a floor only, but rich accumulations of well-trodden dirt.... Having a shutter at one end of the room, if no window, it would be ungrateful to complain of the absence of both door and window-shutter at the other end!"

SCRIPTURE TESTIMONY

Afflictions borne for the Gospel are light and momentary

2 CORINTHIANS 4:7-18

Instead of complaint, the hardships of the campaign were greeted with a smile. It was in the same droll fashion he depicted his own first dwelling-place at Hangchow, where the *Lammermuir* party had found refuge.

> "It is pretty cold weather to be living in a house without any ceiling, and with very few walls and windows! There is a deficiency in the wall of my own bedroom, six feet by nine, closed in with a sheet, so that ventilation is decidedly free! [We can imagine the twinkle in his eye as this was penned. But then follows the more solemn aspect.] But we heed these things very little. Around us are poor dark heathen, large cities without any missionary; populous towns without any missionary; villages without number, all destitute of the means of grace. I do not envy the state of mind that would forget these, or leave them to perish, for fear of a little discomfort."

It must be acknowledged that such conditions constituted a somewhat stern school for new arrivals, especially for any not cast in his Spartan mould. And as these pioneers pressed forward into new centres, and found that scarcely any station was opened without a riot, one or two fell to criticizing their leader. It was just this that Hudson Taylor had feared before his surrender at Brighton.

His forecast had been correct, and it was well that it had already been faced and conquered. But the ordeal was severe, more severe than had been anticipated. Ready ears were lent to the complaints by some who did not approve of Hudson Taylor's methods, and reports reached home which might well have wrecked the young Mission had it not been founded upon the Rock. But it called for faith to be patient under misrepresentation, to be meek when misunderstood and maligned, to refrain from self-assertion, and to await God's vindication. It was not the first time he and his noble wife— who was indeed his "companion in tribulation and in the kingdom and patience of Jesus Christ"—had been in this school of discipline, and their experience before marriage helped them now.

> "It was a marvel," wrote Mrs. Taylor, recalling that time, "that *my* mind even was not poisoned against my dear husband; and we could have no communication with one another, so as to hear the other side. Yet God mercifully kept us from being influenced by the aspersions; and the remembrance of His past dealings must reassure us now."

There was comfort also to be found in the experience of Moses, the meekest of men, under similar provocation, but more especially in the example of the Master, "who when He was reviled, reviled not again; when He suffered, He threatened not; but committed Himself to Him that judgeth righteously." Hudson Taylor's power quietly to wait at such times as these brings out the strong contrast of his nature, his aggressive spirit in the work of God, and his enduring spirit in the realm of suffering. Patience is, as Chrysostom has said, "the King of Virtues."

"Blessed Adversity" was Hudson Taylor's title to an article he wrote in which he deals with trials of this nature.

"The believer does not need to wait until he sees the reason of God's afflictive dealings with him ere he is satisfied; he knows that all things work together for good to them that love God; that all God's dealings are those of a loving Father, who only permits that which for the time being is grievous in order to accomplish results that cannot be achieved in any less painful way. The wise and trustful child of God rejoices in tribulation.... Our Heavenly Father delights to *trust a trustworthy child with a trial* in which he can bring glory to God, and through which he will receive permanent enlargement of heart and blessing for himself and others."

It was this determination to see God only in every trial, and not to look at second causes, that was his strength. It was his faith in God over all, through all, and in all, that gave him the victory. And he was prepared to wait God's time of deliverance, believing, to quote a quaint expression of one of the Pilgrim Fathers: "God outshoots Satan oftentimes in his own bow."

It is easy to read such words, but they fundamentally affect the life of the man who believes them. And Hudson Taylor did believe them. It was the audacity of faith in tribulation. Such trials and such opposition only spurred him to fresh effort to advance God's Kingdom. The best defence was to advance. And from the beginning he had laid his plans for such advance. In his own words:

"All the operations of the Mission are systematic and methodical; and in accordance with, and integral parts of, one general and comprehensive plan for *the evangelization of the whole of China*"

Here was an audacious plan indeed. To those who did not know the secret of his mind he was accused of encouraging "aimless wanderings." But he had not studied the map of China so long in vain. His policy from the first was to seek an opening in the capital of a province, though it was well known that that was the most difficult place in which to gather a Church. His next step was to open stations in the prefectures, and then in subordinate cities. The chief reasons for this procedure were that the subordinate officials would be afraid and unfriendly if the higher officials had not countenanced the foreigner, and it was anticipated that with Churches in the cities the villages would be more easily influenced than *vice versa*.

That the large *Lammermuir* party should have secured a settlement in Hangchow, the capital of Chekiang, was a great point gained. And many would have been satisfied with such substantial progress at the early stages of so young a Mission, but Hudson Taylor was insatiable. He was fired with a passion to possess China for Christ, a passion which burned with an intensity not less than that which consumed the most ambitious conqueror of kingdoms. Napoleon, for instance, after having secured the gates of the Alps in his Piedmont campaign, thus addressed his troops:

> "You have gained battles without cannon, passed rivers without bridges, performed forced marches without shoes, bivouacked without strong liquors, and often without bread. Thanks for your perseverance! But, soldiers, you have done nothing—for there remains much to do."

In a higher cause Hudson Taylor possessed a like spirit. His eye was ever on the great undone. He was never content to rest in the achieved.

And so it was he chose as the watchword for the new year 1867, the first new year after the arrival of the *Lammermuir* party, the Prayer of Jabez: "Oh that Thou wouldst bless me indeed and enlarge my coast, and that Thine hand might be with me, and that Thou wouldst keep me from the evil, that it may not grieve me!" And it was a remarkable fact that by the end of that year, or only a little more than twelve months from the arrival of that party at Hangchow, there were China Inland missionaries resident in six of the eleven prefectural cities of Chekiang, including the capital, while a seventh prefectural city was opened, though with no one actually in residence, and the pioneer Duncan was also established in Nanking, the capital of another province, Kiangsu. Thus the young Mission had already eight stations, in two provinces, all prefectural cities, and the most remote, twenty-four days apart. And there were, in all, thirty-four missionaries in the field. The prayer of Jabez had certainly been heard.

But his cry was still "On, on to do my Father's business." The immeasurable need urged him on.

> "My thoughts are busied," he wrote, "now with the untold need of the unoccupied provinces, now with the neglected districts of this province (Chekiang), until I am compelled to roll the burden on the Lord, and cry to Him for wisdom to dispose aright of those He may send to help me, and to plead for more Chinese and foreign workers."

But, in his eagerness for advance, he did not forget the spiritual needs of his own fellow-soldiers. In one of his letters to his mother he speaks of rising before daylight, for quiet waiting upon God for every member of the Mission. This was his constant practice. He once acknowledged to a friend that the sun had never risen upon China without finding him either praying for, or having prayed for, those labouring with him on the field. He was a strong believer in "the morning watch."

On the 30th May, 1867, he wrote to Mr. Berger:

> "More than a year has elapsed since we parted on the deck of the *Lammermuir,* but both you and I can still say—of the past, *Ebenezer;* of the present, *Jehovah-Nissi;* and of the future, *Jehovah-Jireh;* thanks be to His grace!

"Burdens such as I never before sustained, responsibilities such as I had not hitherto incurred, and sorrows compared with which all my past sorrows were light have been part of my experience. But I trust I have, in some feeble measure, learned more of the blessed truth, that

> "'Sufficient is His arm alone.
> And our defence is sure.'"

The watchwords quoted above prove whence came his audacity of faith. He had set God ever before him, that he should not be moved. It was God behind, God present, and God before.

XVII

LIKE AS A FATHER

I T IS one of the most amazing and yet, at the same time, one of the most illuminating truths that God made man in His own image. Things fundamentally human must therefore be Godlike, since He made us after His own likeness. And it is written: "Male *and* female created He them," from which statement, and from many another Scripture, confirmed by Christ Himself, man has the authority for the belief that the father-heart *and* the mother-heart are both reflections of the heart of God Himself. And the man who knows best what the father's heart really is will find it easiest to take the place of the child. And Hudson Taylor, in no small measure, became the man he did because he had a sufficiently sanctified imagination to learn to know God through those relationships which are fundamentally human.

Hudson Taylor was no ascetic, devoid of natural affection; indeed, nature as well as grace had richly endowed him in this respect. What he was as son and brother, many volumes of letters, still extant, abundantly prove. And when he became a husband and a father, a new and deep fount of love welled up and overflowed toward wife and children. And since he knew that every family in heaven and on earth receives its name and nature from the Father of our Lord above, he had only to look into his own heart to see the mirrored image of the great heart of God Himself. There was no title he more loved to use for God than "Father." And there was no attitude he more rejoiced to adopt than that of a trustful child. No one can understand Hudson Taylor, as he really was, without recognizing that all life's family relationships spoke to him of those eternal realities of which they are the types. From the shadows of the Heavenlies he sought to grasp the "very image."

Of all his devotional writings none has had so wide a circulation as his little commentary on the *Song of Songs,* published under the title of *Union and Communion.* Here we find Hudson Taylor as one of the true Mystics of the Church, as the very title of the book suggests. And there can be no doubt but that this little book, in which he reveals his heart possibly more than in any other of his writings, owed not a little to the joy and satisfaction he had found in his own wedded love. And as children came and awakened the dormant wealth of his parental affection, this also in its turn became to him a fresh revelation of the heart of the Eternal.

SCRIPTURE TESTIMONY

Our Father in heaven gives good things

MATTHEW 7:9-11

His first-born child was little Gracie, born as we have seen in China on July 31, 1859. Three sons, Herbert Hudson, Frederick Howard, and Samuel Dyer, were born during his five and a half years in England, while another daughter, Maria Hudson, was given them in February, 1867, shortly after their arrival in Hangchow To launch forth into the heart of China with such parental responsibilities was not lightly undertaken. Hudson Taylor was not blind to the stern realities of life, but every exercise of his heart in these matters only confirmed his confidence in the love and care of his Heavenly Father.

> "I am taking my children with me," he wrote shortly before leaving England, "and I notice that it is not difficult for me to remember that the little ones need breakfast in the morning, dinner at midday, and something before they go to bed at night. Indeed I *could* not forget it. And I find it *impossible* to suppose that our Heavenly Father is less tender or mindful than I."

This was the literal and practical way in which he took heart from Christ's words: "If ye then being evil, know how to give good gifts unto your children, how much more shall your Father which is in Heaven give good things to them that ask Him?" This truth he loved to dwell upon, especially when responsibilities were great.

> "I do not believe," he wrote, "that our Heavenly Father will ever forget His children. I am a very poor father, but it is not my habit to forget my children. God is a very, very good Father. It is not His habit to forget His children."

It seems all so simple, but it was truth which plumbed the depths of reality. It reveals the heart of the child, it is true, but that appeals to and calls forth all the resources of the Father.

A glimpse into his own fatherly heart may be obtained by the recital of a little incident which he has recorded in detail in one of his books now out of print. His little daughter Maria, when only five years of age, brought him on his birthday a self-made present, in preference to a bought one. What the little gift was intended to be he was at a loss to know, for it consisted of a small piece of wood, in which a peg had been inserted with half a cockle-shell hung on the top. That he might not grieve the child by any failure to recognize the gift, he took her on his knee and engaged her in conversation. And it proved to be intended for a ship to take him back to China!

It was a small thing, and might easily have been forgotten by a busy man, but thirty-five years later, when he was writing his little volume *Separation and Service,* he devoted two and a half pages to recording this incident, just to illustrate God's pleasure in the love-gifts of His children. Referring to his child's words: "I thought you would like best a ship to take you to China," he added:

> "The dear child was right; probably no gift I ever received gave more pleasure, or was more carefully treasured and as often thought of."

And then, from his own emotions, arguing up to God, he said:

> "It is not hard to please those we love. God is not hard to please, nor is human love, for it is a dim reflection of His own. We do not

estimate our love-gifts by their intrinsic value, but rather by the love they express." And then he continues: "God *wants our love.* He wants our *sympathy;* He wants the gifts and offerings which are prompted by *love.* Shall He look to us in vain? Our David still thirsts, not for the waters of the well of Bethlehem, but for the souls for which He died. Shall He not have them?"

This child-like attitude of heart played so large a part in the life of Hudson Taylor that one more incident must be given as related by Dr. Harry Guinness. Hudson Taylor was seated in the Doctor's study at Harley House.

> "I shall never forget seeing him sit back in the armchair," said Harry Guinness, "evidently very tired and evidently very much appreciating the little rest. My mother was speaking to him, and I had a little child in my arms, and was walking quietly up and down the room. My mother said: 'Dear friend, I suppose that sometimes you must find the burden of the Mission almost intolerable.' He looked up and said, 'Oh no, Mrs. Guinness, no, never, never.' Then, pointing over to me, he said, 'Do you think that your son would see the little one in his arms suffering need if he had a crust left? Think you not that he would give it?' I never can forget that," said Dr. Guinness, "nor the calm and beautiful way in which he then gave testimony to a peace which passeth understanding."

He believed, not as a beautiful sentiment, but as an unchangeable reality, that "Like as a father pitieth his children so the Lord pitieth them that fear Him" This was the secret of his strength and peace, and this calm trustfulness in God as a Father was one of the greatest legacies he left behind him. And when he spoke of God as a Father he did not forget the more tender affection we associate with a mother's love. Writing on Numbers vii., one of the longest chapters in the Bible, all devoted to offerings given to God, he said:

"Does not the full detail of this chapter reveal the love and tenderness of Him whose Book it is towards each offerer, and bring out what we may reverently call the Mother-side of God's character. Who has condescended to say: 'As one whom his mother comforteth, so will I comfort you.'"

In a New Year's Address, entitled *Under the Shepherd's Care,* he records an incident to which he constantly made reference.

"I have frequently thought of words I had the privilege of hearing some years ago from Professor Charteris at a united Communion service for students in Edinburgh. He said that there had been one life on earth of steady, uninterrupted development from the cradle to the Cross; but that there had only been one such life, for true Christian life always began where the life of Christ ended, *at the Cross;* and that its true development is *towards the cradle,* until the child of God in the childlike simplicity of faith can rest in the omnipotent arms of infinite Wisdom and Love."

And now we are permitted to accompany this man, so intensely human as well as so eminently spiritual, into the secret chamber where he was sorely stricken in the tenderest spot of his nature. And it may be remarked in passing that what most men find it difficult, if not impossible, to do, Hudson Taylor could and did do, and that was to admit the outsider into the sacred realm of his own heart. It is one explanation of his influence with and over men; he was no mere official, but a man of like passions with others, not ashamed to reveal genuine emotion.

At the beginning of 1867 he had written:

"I have long felt that our Mission has a baptism to be baptized with. It may not yet be passed. It may be heavier than we can foresee. But if, by grace, we are kept faithful, in the end all will be well."

These words, written shortly after the death of one of the *Lammermuir* party, appear like a premonition of what was to befall the leader of the Mission himself. For all God's waves and billows were to pass over him, but only to prove the truth of the promise that the waters should not overflow or overwhelm.

The summer of that year was intensely hot, the thermometer indoors being frequently above 100° F. All the children suffered, and Mrs. Taylor was also ill, so that a trip to the neighbouring hills was arranged. The change from the sultry city to the beauty and the comparative freshness of the country was an intense relief, but it did not suffice to do all that had been hoped. Little Gracie, the darling of her parents, sickened with a fatal disease, and Hudson Taylor, when writing to Mr. Berger on August 15, 1867, unburdened his heart as follows:

> "I know not how to write to you, nor how to refrain. I seem to be writing almost from the inner chamber of the King of kings— surely this is holy ground. I am striving to write a few lines from the side of a couch on which my darling Gracie lies dying. Her complaint is hydrocephalus. Dear brother, our flesh and heart fail, but God is the strength of our heart and our portion for ever. It was no vain nor unintelligent act, when knowing the land, its people and climate, I laid my dear wife and the darling children with myself on the altar for this service. And He whom so unworthily, and with much weakness and failure, we are and have been endeavouring to serve in simplicity and godly sincerity, has not left us. *Ebenezer* and *Jehovah-Jireh* are still dear words to us."

The dread complaint rapidly ran its course, and on the 29th he wrote again:

"The Lord has taken our sweet little Gracie to bloom in the purer atmosphere of His own presence. Our hearts *bleed;* but

> "'Above the rest this note shall swell—
> Our Jesus hath done all things well.'"

Writing a little later to his own mother at home, who had also known the loss of loved children, he added:

> "Our torn hearts will revert to the one subject, and I know not how to write to you of any other. Our dear little Gracie! How we miss her sweet voice in the morning, one of the first sounds to greet us when we woke—and through the day and at eventide! As I take the walks I used to take with her tripping at my side, the thought comes anew like a throb of agony, 'Is it possible

that I shall never more feel the pressure of that little hand, never more hear the sweet prattle of those dear lips, never more see the sparkle of those bright eyes?' And yet she is not *lost*. I would not have her back again."

And Gracie's mother, though with a rent heart, accepted this poignant sorrow in the same spirit. Father and mother were one in this. There was no repining, no looking back, only a determination to trust unerring love. The more that sorrow revealed the depths of their own love, the more it manifested to them the heart of Him who so loved the world as to give His only Son. Not long before he had written to his mother:

> "It is an easy thing to sing, 'I all on earth forsake.' It Is not very difficult to think, and honestly though ignorantly to say, 'I give up *all* to Thee, and for Thee.' But God sometimes teaches one that that little word *'all'* is terribly comprehensive."

The value of Hudson Taylor's testimony lies in the fact that terribly comprehensive as it proved to be the refining fire revealed only genuine gold and not the dross of self-deception. Hudson Taylor's simple, childlike faith stood all the stem tests of an exacting life and heart-rending sorrows, and he still continued "stedfast, unmovable, always abounding in the work of the Lord." He never could exhaust the infinite wealth of those simple words: "Like as a father."

XVIII

IT IS THE LORD

IT WAS not long after the death of little Gracie that Hudson Taylor decided upon a forward movement into the heart of China. All thought of repining was alien to his faith in God, and never did any man more resolutely cultivate the cheerful spirit. Within two months of Gracie's death he wrote home:

> "Amid heavy trials we have had abundant blessings, and so many obvious answers to special prayers, that it is with thankful hearts we go forward."

And the following lines, quoted in the third edition of *China's Spiritual Need and Claims,* under date of Hangchow, 1868, reveal his mind at that time.

> "Who spoke of rest? There is a rest above.
> No rest on earth for me. On, on to do
> My Father's business. He, who sent me here.
> Appointed me my time on earth to bide,
> And set me all my work to do for Him,
> He will supply me with sufficient grace—
> Grace to be doing, to be suffering.
> Not to be resting. There is rest above."

Though no man knew better how to rest in the Lord, there was ever a note of urgency about Hudson Taylor. He felt he was, to use a phrase of his own, engaged in "a race of time against eternity." This finds illustration in the Preface to the third edition of the little book just mentioned. In this he wrote:

"Let us urge the reader solemnly to consider the weighty facts contained in the following pages, and whatever his hand findeth to do, to do it with his might; for not only is the night coming, in which no man can work, but opportunities—precious opportunities—are fast passing away, never to recur. [And then referring to the rebuilding of temples after the rebellion, he continues.] And wounded hearts, that might have joyfully accepted the message of God's love, are turning again to the wretched husks which Satan—less dull to see, and less slow to improve his opportunities—is again foisting upon them."

When Hudson Taylor penned those words: "On, on to do my Father's business," he gave vent to more than a pious expression, for at the same time he pulled up the tent-pegs of his own home at Hangchow, and set forth with wife and family for the heart of China. As leader he took his place in the vanguard.

The tedious battle with difficulties which followed his arrival on the Yangtse cannot be told in detail. After wearying and fruitless negotiations over some thirty houses in Yangchow, one was at length rented on July 17, 1868, and Hudson Taylor and family, with thankful hearts, took possession. Midsummer heat in the Valley of the Yangtse is distressing enough, without the added burden of house-hunting. But difficulties at Chinkiang were more formidable than at Yangchow owing to the bitterly anti-foreign animosity of the local Mandarin. Not only did he rebuff all Hudson Taylor's efforts to secure premises, but he checkmated the kindly offices of the British Consul. His success in frustrating the foreigner soon became the talk of the tea-shops, and that encouraged the baser sort at Yangchow to plot the ejection of the newly-arrived missionary party.

It is not possible in a few words to convey any adequate sense of the acute anxiety of the weeks that followed, or of the anguish of the actual riot. Most things must be experienced to be appreciated. By means of vile and evil reports the minds of the people were in-flamed against the strangers in their midst. On August 22, it was stated, and believed, that as many as twenty- two Chinese children were missing, with the result that the Mission premises were besieged by an infuriated mob. All

> **SCRIPTURE TESTIMONY**
>
> *Believers accused through testimony of false witness*
>
> MATTHEW 26:59 · MARK 14:55-59 · ACTS 6:9-14

through the night that followed, and the next day as well, every moment was full of acute suspense and mental anguish, not to speak of much physical pain.

Hudson Taylor and George Duncan had, under cover of darkness, evaded the howling multitude, and, though badly stoned, reached the Yamen, more than a mile away, in an exhausted condition. But there they were detained, in an agony of suspense, for hours, while they could hear, in the distance, pandemonium let loose around the Mission premises. Whether their loved ones were alive or dead they did not know, and neither did those left in the Mission House know what had befallen those who had ventured forth.

But the maddened people were not satisfied with cries and threats, and the cowardly inaction of the official emboldened them at length to fire the premises. To escape became now a necessity, but a perilous undertaking. Mrs. Taylor and Miss Blatchley both had to jump from the upper storey, and both were injured in so doing, while Mr. Reid when endeavouring to break their fall was struck in the eye with a brick which left him almost blind with pain. For nearly forty-eight hours this typhoon of human fury raged, far more terrible than any storm at sea, and only the infinite mercy of God brought the party through, though wounded and bleeding, without serious loss of life.

The spirit in which these indignities and sufferings were borne is best illustrated by a few extracts from letters of that period. Mrs. Taylor wrote:

> **SCRIPTURE TESTIMONY**
>
> *Afflictions borne for the Gospel are light and momentary*
>
> 2 CORINTHIANS 4:7-18

"I had felt encouraged to hope that help was at hand, by the fact that my own strength was rapidly ebbing away from loss of blood. I was anxious not to let anyone know how much I was hurt, as I felt it would alarm them, and it seemed most important that all should keep calm.

"My heart was too full to pay much heed to the scene of ruin through which we passed, but at the foot of the stair my eye fell on a bead mat worked for me by our little Gracie before leaving England. The sight of it at that moment seemed to speak of our Father's love and tenderness in a way that perhaps it would be difficult for another to understand." [It was just a year to the very day since her death.]

In another letter she added:

"The faithful and tender love that preserved all our lives and restored us to each other at that terrible time will, I trust, inspire us with fresh confidence in the future.... I shall count all our physical sufferings light, and our mental anxieties, severe though they were, well repaid, if they may work out for the further opening of the country to us for the spread of our Master's Kingdom."

Such extracts, and there is much more that could be quoted, reveal what manner of woman Mrs. Hudson Taylor was. How her husband was affected the following few lines will show:

"We are not disappointed, we are not daunted. We expected to meet with difficulties, but we counted on God's help and protection, and so far from being disheartened, we take courage from the goodness of God to us in our extreme peril; and from the very opposition of Satan, are the more determined to continue the conflict."

Instead of allowing difficulties and opposition to daunt him, he even drew encouragement from them, as the Apostle Paul did from afflictions.

"If God in His providence order that our work shall lead to valleys of difficulty which we cannot bridge over, to mountain obstacles which we have no means of surmounting, to crooked paths which the united zeal and energy of the Church cannot make straight, to rough places that no human power can make plain, shall we be discouraged? Shall we not bless and praise His Holy Name for a clear platform on which His holy arm, ever working, though hiddenly, can be made bare—on which all flesh, and not merely the enlightened believer, must see the manifestation of the glory of the Lord? From this point of view our difficulties are seen to be for our greatest good, and our best ground for encouragement."

Of the attack upon the Mission at home, both by the Press and Parliament, we must not speak. That had mainly to be faced by Mr. Berger. What more concerns us here was Hudson Taylor's attitude towards such manifestations of Satanic fury. The secret of his rest of heart, amid such tempests of hate, was his refusal to look at second causes. His times were in God's hands. He believed that it was with God, and God alone, he had to do. This is strikingly brought out in his article entitled *Blessed Adversity*. With the experiences of Job as his text, he wrote:

"Even Satan did not presume to ask God to be allowed *himself* to afflict Job. In the 1st chapter and the nth verse he says: 'Put forth *Thine* hand now, and touch all that he hath, and he will curse Thee to Thy face.' And in the 2nd chapter and the 5th verse: 'Put forth *Thine* hand now, and touch his bone and his flesh, and he will curse Thee to Thy face.' Satan knew that *none but God* could touch Job; and when Satan was permitted to afflict him, Job was quite right in recognizing the Lord Himself as the doer of these things which He permitted to be done.

"Oftentimes shall we be helped and blessed if we bear this in mind—that Satan is *servant,* and not *master,* and that he and wicked men incited by him are only permitted to do that which God by His determinate counsel and foreknowledge has before determined shall be done. Come joy, or come sorrow, we may always take it from the hand of God.

"Judas betrayed his Master with a kiss. Our Lord did not stop short at Judas, nor did He even stop short at the great enemy who filled the heart of Judas to do this thing; but He said: 'the cup which *My FATHER* hath given Me, shall I not drink it?'

"How the tendency to resentment and a wrong feeling would be removed, could we take an injury from the hand of a loving Father, instead of looking chiefly at the agent through whom it comes to us! It matters not who is the postman—it is with the writer of the letter that we are concerned; it matters not who is the messenger—it is with God that His children have to do.

"We conclude, therefore, that Job was not mistaken, and that we shall not be mistaken if we follow his example, in accepting all God's providential dealings as from Himself. We may be sure that they will issue in ultimate blessing; because God is GOD, and therefore, 'all things work together for good to them that love Him.'"

Such a passage as this shows how invulnerable was his position. He had taken to himself the Shield of Faith—not the small wieldy buckler which left the fighter largely exposed, but the full-length shield— wherewith to quench all the fiery darts of the evil one. By faith he stood, and by faith he advanced.

We cannot relate in detail the course of events during the months that followed the riot. In November of the same year he was reinstated, but meanwhile he had been breaking new ground to the north of the province, and subsequently he was busy visiting the older stations. The Mission during 1869 gained a footing in two new provinces, Anhwei and Kiangsi, but for the purposes of our story this year was most memorable for the great spiritual blessing which came to Hudson Taylor. The Lord whom he sought suddenly came to His temple, even the Messenger of the Covenant whom he delighted in. But that experience demands a chapter to itself. We must here pass on, with uncovered heads, into the valley of the shadow of death whither Hudson Taylor's steps were bound. The point to note is, that whatever came, his heart still said: "It is the Lord, let Him do what seemeth to Him good." He sometimes expressed his convictions in these words:

> "With peaceful mind thy path of duty run:
> God nothing does, nor suffers to be done,
> But what thou wouldst thyself, could thou but see
> The end of all events as well as He."

Such words can easily be quoted when life's path is smooth, but it is another matter when hard beset by trial and temptation. How the iron had entered his soul the following passage, in which he opens his heart to his mother at this time, will help to show:

> "Envied of some, despised by many, hated perhaps by others; often blamed for things I never heard of, or had nothing to do with; an innovator on what have become established rules of missionary practice; an opponent of mighty systems of heathen error and superstitions; working without precedent in many respects, and with few experienced helpers; often sick in body, as well as perplexed in mind and embarrassed by circumstances; had not the Lord been specially gracious to me, had not my mind been sustained by the conviction that the work is His, and that He is with me in what it is no empty figure to call 'the thick of the conflict,' I must have fainted and broken down. But the battle is the Lord's: and He will conquer. We may fail, do fail continually; but He never fails."

It was well that he had been spiritually refreshed during 1869, for 1870 was a year filled with, humanly speaking, overwhelming sorrows and anxieties. Early in the year, Mr. and Mrs. Taylor had to face the break up of their home, for it was all too evident that the elder children must leave the country before the great heat came. Arrangements were therefore made for the four eldest, Herbert, Howard, Samuel and Maria, to sail with Miss Blatchley, while the youngest, Charles, was to remain with his parents. This separation was keenly felt, and was, to quote Hudson Taylor's words, "a dark cloud" which seemed "to take all one's strength away." And the cloud was darker than he thought, for ere the children sailed, little Samuel, the youngest member of the *Lammermuir* party, suddenly sickened and died, and was laid to rest in the cemetery at Chinkiang.

Toward the close of March the stricken parents bade farewell to the other three, little knowing they were never again to meet on earth as a united family. Then in addition to this personal sorrow came keen anxiety about the whole situation in China. There had been Mohammedan rebellions in the far south-west and far north-west. Russia had entered Chinese Turkestan, and the wildest rumours were believed concerning the designs of foreigners generally. Deep and widespread excitement shook the very foundations of Chinese society, which culminated in the terrible massacre, at Tientsin in June, of ten Sisters of Mercy, the French Consul, several other Frenchmen, and several Russians believed to be French.

As all this happened just as the Franco-Prussian War broke out, France was helpless to intervene. To the Chinese the humiliation of France before Germany was a proof of her guilt and of Heaven's vengeance, so that the tide of anti-foreign animosity threatened to rise higher still. At Nanking the Viceroy was assassinated, and no one knew whereunto things would grow.

It was inevitable that, at such a time, Hudson Taylor's anxieties and responsibilities concerning the workers up country should be great and onerous.

> "Almost daily," he said, "I had letters from some group of workers asking for guidance, and wondering whether to stay or leave the station, as work for the time being was impossible. I knew not what to advise, but in each case, like Hezekiah, I spread the letters before the Lord, and trusted Him to teach me how to reply to them. There was no conscious revelation, but in every instance I was guided to reply in the way that led to the best results, and I sent each letter off in the joyful peace of knowing that I had asked, and He had granted, the wisdom that is profitable to direct."

The Tientsin massacre was in June, as already mentioned. Such workers as had had to leave their stations were gathered together at Chinkiang, where the Mission premises were uncomfortably crowded. Here on July 5 Mrs. Taylor was seized with cholera. Two days later a son, their fifth son, Noel, was born, but the mother was too weak to nurse her babe. Thirteen days later the little one breathed his last, and on the 23rd, at daybreak, the beloved mother also passed beyond earth's shadows.

For twelve and a half years Mrs. Taylor had been the light and joy of her husband's eyes, and a Mother in Israel to the Mission. Endowed with gifts and graces beyond the

SCRIPTURE TESTIMONY
We do not grieve as those who have no hope
I THESSALONIANS 4:13

average, well versed in Chinese literature and customs, full of faith and courage, she had been a tower of strength both to Hudson Taylor and to the Mission. And what was even more, her quiet daily walk with God had set the spiritual standard high for all who knew her. In answer to a question, she said to her husband, on the very morning she died: "You know, darling, that for ten years past there has not been a cloud between me and my Saviour. I cannot be sorry to go to Him: but it does grieve me to leave you alone at such a time."

In this Valley of Deep Darkness, Hudson Taylor proved God's grace sufficient, and was made more than conqueror. From his heart he said: "The Lord gave, and the Lord hath taken away; blessed be the Name of the Lord." This was said deliberately, and on those words he subsequently added this comment:

> "Was not Job mistaken? Should he not have said: 'the Lord gave, and Satan hath taken away'? No, there was no mistake. The same grace which had enabled him unharmed to receive blessing from God enabled him also to discern the hand of God in the calamities which had befallen him."

Writing to his mother some ten days after his great loss he said:

> "My views are not changed, though chastened and deepened. From my inmost soul I delight in the knowledge that God does or deliberately permits all things, and causes all things to work together for good to those who love Him.

"He, and He only, knew what my dear wife was to me. He knew how the light of my eyes and the joy of my heart were in her.... But He saw that it was good to take her; good indeed for her, and in His love He took her painlessly; and not less good for me who must henceforth toil and suffer alone—yet not alone, for God is nearer to me than ever."

"Did not we cast three men bound into the midst of the fire?" said Nebuchadnezzar to his counsellors. "They answered and said unto the king, 'true, O king.' Then answered Nebuchadnezzar: 'Lo, I see four men loose, walking in the midst of the fire, and they have no hurt; and the form of the fourth is like the Son of God.'" And Hudson Taylor's experience was not dissimilar, for the Son of God was with him in his furnace of sorrow.

"I scarcely knew," he wrote, "whether she or I was the more blessed, so real, so constant, so satisfying was His Presence, so deep my delight in the consciousness that His will was being done, and that that Will, which was utterly crushing me, was good, and wise, and best."

XIX

THE ETERNAL SPRINGS OF GOD

T HAT HUDSON Taylor was no stranger to Him who is the "hidden Source of calm repose," our "Light in Satan's darkest hour," has already been abundantly apparent. But we must now go back a few months, and dwell upon that rich spiritual experience into which he had entered nearly a year before the death of his wife.

From the beginning of 1869 he had been deeply dissatisfied with his spiritual condition. He was oppressed by a sense of failure, and of living below his privileged inheritance. There was probably more than one reason for this. It is instructive to note that in England the subject of personal holiness had been taking a prominent place in the minds of God's people. All through the summer and autumn of 1868 many articles on this topic had appeared in the columns of *The Revival*, now known as *The Christian*. These papers would come into Hudson Taylor's hands toward the latter part of the year.

There was also a little booklet entitled *How to live on Christ*, by Mrs. Harriet Beecher Stowe, which had so deeply moved Hudson Taylor as to cause him to send a copy of it to every member of the Mission. How far his sense of failure was independent of, or related to, his reading it is perhaps impossible now to say. But there is no question that he was reading a good deal on this subject at this time, for another book in his library, entitled *Christ is All,* was not only blessed to one of his fellow-workers, but also indirectly to himself. But be the cause what it may, it is clear that the Spirit of God, who was moving upon the hearts of His people at home, was also doing a similar work in China, for at this time not a few members of the Mission entered into a new enjoyment of fulness of life in Christ. But in Hudson Taylor's case the entrance into liberty and joy was preceded by months of bondage and almost despair. Writing to his mother in the spring of 1869 he said:

> "I cannot tell you how I am buffeted sometimes by temptation. I never knew how bad a heart I had.... Often I am tempted to think that one so full of sin cannot be a child of God at all; but I try to throw it back, and rejoice all the more in the preciousness of Jesus."

When writing to his sister Amelia (Mrs. Benjamin Broomhall), in the autumn of the same year, he alluded to the same subject.

SCRIPTURE TESTIMONY
Believers are in Jesus, and He is in them
JOHN 15:1-17

"My mind," he wrote, "has been greatly exercised for six or eight months past, feeling the need personally, and for our Mission, of more holiness, life, power in our souls. But personal need stood first and was the greatest. I felt the ingratitude, the danger, the sin of not living near to God. I prayed diligently, sought more time for retirement and meditation—but all was without effect. Every day, almost every hour, the consciousness of sin oppressed me.... Each day brought its register of sin and failure. To will was indeed present with me, but how to perform I knew not.

"Then came the question: 'Is there no rescue? Must it be thus to the end?' ...I hated myself; I hated my sin; and yet I gained no strength against it.... Hope itself almost died out, and I began to think that, perhaps to make Heaven the sweeter, God would not give it down here."

It was when the agony of his soul was at its height that he received a letter from his fellow-worker John M'Carthy, who had been passing through a somewhat similar experience, but had been brought out into the light. Writing from Hangchow Mr. M'Carthy said:

> "I have been struck with a passage from a book of yours left here, entitled *Christ is All.* It says:
>
> "'The Lord Jesus received is holiness begun; the Lord Jesus cherished is holiness advancing; the Lord Jesus counted upon as never absent would be holiness complete.'"

Commenting on this passage and its context, Mr. M'Carthy said that he felt as "though the first dawning of a glorious day had risen upon him." And then he continued—and these were the lines which specially helped Hudson Taylor:

> "How then to have our faith increased? Only by thinking of all that Jesus is, and all He is for us. His life, His death. His work, He Himself as revealed to us in the Word, to be the subject of our constant thoughts. Not a striving to have faith, or to increase our faith, but a looking off to the Faithful One, seems all we need; a resting in the Loved One entirely, for time and eternity. It does not appear to me as anything new, only formerly misapprehended."

When Hudson Taylor reached his home at Chinkiang on Saturday, September 4, after a visit to Yangchow, he found this letter awaiting him. Opening it he read, and as he read, the vision he had needed flashed upon him. It was to his thirsty soul as living water from the Eternal Springs of God. But, as he must speak for himself, we continue to quote his letter to his sister.

> "As I read I saw it all! 'If we believe *not;* He abideth faithful.' I looked to Jesus and saw (and when I saw, oh, how the joy flowed!) that He had said: *'I* will never leave *you.'* 'Ah, *there* is rest,' I thought. 'I have striven in vain to rest in Him. I'll strive no more. For has *He* not promised to abide with me—never to leave me, never to fail me?' And, dearie, *He never will.*

"But this was not all He showed me, nor one half. As I thought of the Vine and the branches, what light the blessed Spirit poured direct into my soul! How great seemed my mistake in having wished to get the sap, the fulness out of Him. I saw not only that Jesus would never leave me, but that I was a member of His body, of His flesh and of His bones. The Vine now I see is not the root merely, but all —root, stem, branches, twigs, leaves, flowers, fruit: and Jesus is not only that: He is soil and sunshine, air and showers, and ten thousand times more than we have ever dreamed, wished for, or needed. Oh, the joy of seeing this truth!

> **SCRIPTURE TESTIMONY**
>
> *The believer remains in Christ,*
> *and Christ lives in the believer*
>
> JOHN 15:1-6 · JOHN 15:1-17

"Oh, my dear sister, it is a wonderful thing to be really one with a risen and exalted Saviour; to be a member of Christ! Think what it involves. Can Christ be rich and I poor?...

"The sweetest part, if one may speak of one part being sweeter than another, is the *rest* that full identification with Christ brings. I am no longer anxious about anything, as I realize this; for He, I know, is able to carry out *His Will,* and His Will is mine....

"I feel and know that old things have passed away. I am as capable of sinning as ever, but Christ is realized as present as never before. He cannot sin; and He can keep me from sinning. I cannot say (I am sorry to have to confess it) that since I have seen this light I have not sinned; but I do feel there is no need to have done so. And further—walking more in the light, my conscience has been more tender; sin has been instantly seen, confessed, pardoned; and peace and joy (with humility) instantly restored; with one exception, when for several hours peace and joy did not return—from want, as I had to learn, of full confession, and from some attempt to justify self.

"Faith, I now see, is '*the substance* of things hoped for,' and not a mere shadow. It is not *less* than sight, but *more.* Sight only shows the outward form of things; faith gives the substance. You can *rest* on substance, feed on substance. Christ dwelling in the heart by faith (*i.e.* His Word of Promise credited) is *power* indeed, is *life* indeed."

This was not merely sentiment or emotion. The reality of this experience was tested immediately, and to the uttermost. There was at the time a financial stringency of an acute nature, largely arising out of unjust criticism at home of the Mission's responsibility for the Yangchow riot. So urgent did economy become that Mr. Taylor had to dispense with his cook, and have food brought in from a public kitchen, at the cost of only one Mexican dollar per head per month, the dollar being worth about five shillings at that time. That meant twopence a head per day for food! Then there was the riot at Anking, and fear that this might lead to further harsh criticism. Writing to Mr. Berger he said:

"Difficulties greater and more serious than I have ever had *crowd* upon me. The last few months have been of unparalleled pressure and constant movement; but I have enjoyed more leisure of soul and rest of spirit than ever before, and more joy in the Lord. If satisfied with His will and way, *there is rest.*"

That was written in December, 1869, just three months after his newly-found joy. In the following February his little son Samuel died; in March he had to bid farewell to his three eldest children when they sailed for England, in June was the Tientsin massacre, and all its attendant anxieties, and in July, as we have seen, his wife and babe were both taken from him at one blow. And then came sickness—ague, dysentery, and sleeplessness. Stripped of almost all that was personally precious, it was a more sweeping experience than that portrayed by Habakkuk, when fig-tree, olive, and vine ceased to flourish, and when field, flock, and herd failed. It was more than worldly substance gone, it was his heart's cherished treasure. And yet Hudson Taylor continued to rejoice in God, and to joy in the God of his salvation. His letters which remain bear extraordinary witness to the sustaining and satisfying power of God's grace.

> SCRIPTURE TESTIMONY
>
> *Blessed are those who mourn*
>
> MATTHEW 5:4 · LUKE 6:21

"A few months ago," he wrote to Mr. Berger, "my home was full, now so silent and lonely—Samuel, Noel, my precious wife, with Jesus; the elder children far, far away, and even little T'ien-pao[1] in Yangchow. Often, of late years, has duty called me from my loved ones, but I have returned, and so warm has been the welcome. Now I am alone. Can it be that there is no return from this journey, no home-gathering to look forward to! Is it real, and not a sorrowful dream, that those dearest to me lie beneath the cold sod? Ah, it is indeed true. But not more so than that there is a homecoming awaiting me which no parting shall break into.... Love gave the blow that for a little while makes the desert more dreary, but heaven more home-like."

Or again; in another letter dated three months later:

"He knows what her absence is to me. Twelve years and a half of such unbroken spiritual fellowship, united labour, mutual satisfaction and love, fall to the lot of very few.... But were the blank less, I should know less of His power and sustaining love."

And in another letter, penned on the same day, he wrote:

"No language can express what He has been and is to me. *Never* does He leave me; constantly does He cheer me with His love. He who once wept at the grave of Lazarus often now weeps in and with me.... His own rest, His own peace, His own joy, He gives me. He kisses me with the kisses of His love, which are better than wine. Often I find myself wondering whether it is possible for her, who is taken, to have more joy in His presence than He has given me."

That he recognized that such experiences were supernatural is made abundantly clear by a few words in a letter to Mr. George Müller of Bristol, who also had lost his wife. The letter is dated March, 1871.

---

1   Charles Hudson Taylor.

"*You* do know, beloved brother, what the cup is that I am daily called to drink—yes, many times a day.... The flesh is weak; and your sympathy and prayers I do prize and thank you for. They tell me of Him who, when the poor and needy seek water, *and there is none*—no, not one drop—opens rivers in high places, and fountains in the midst of the valleys."

Yes, when there was no water, not one drop, God did open His Eternal Springs in the deep and dark valley. There was no passage of Scripture more inseparably connected with

> **SCRIPTURE TESTIMONY**
>
> *Those who believe in Jesus shall be filled with the Spirit*
>
> JOHN 4:10 · JOHN 7:37-38

this experience in Hudson Taylor's mind than the Fourth Chapter of St. John's Gospel, where the story of the Samaritan woman and Christ's offer of living water is told. In a little booklet entitled *Unfailing Springs,* published by him many years later, after expounding the passage he added some words of personal testimony.

"One afternoon," he wrote, "in the course of my usual reading, I came to John 4. It had always been ancient history to me, and as such loved and appreciated, but that afternoon, for the first time, it became a present message to my soul. No one could have been more thirsty, and I there and then accepted the gracious invitation, and asked and received the Living Water, believing from His own Word that my thirsty days were all past, not for any present feeling, but because of His promise."

He then related the trials and the sorrows which had come upon him, as we have just seen. He then continues:

"Then I understood why the Lord had made this passage so real to me. An illness of some weeks followed, and oh! how lonesome at times were the weary hours when confined to my bed; how I missed my dear wife, and the little pattering footsteps of the children far away in England. Perhaps twenty times in a day, as I felt the heart-thirst coming back again, I cried to the Lord, 'You promised me that I should never thirst,' and at once the Lord came and more than satisfied my sorrowing heart, so that I often wondered whether it were possible that my loved one who had been taken could be enjoying a fuller revelation of His presence than I in my lonely chamber."

In all this we have another, and a striking, illustration of the way in which Hudson Taylor took God literally at His Word. He would have nothing to do with Mr. Clip-promise. He held fast to God's faithfulness.

"What a promise!" he says. "'SHALL NEVER THIRST.' To *know* that 'shall' means shall; that 'never' means never; that 'thirst' means any unsatisfied need, may be one of the greatest revelations God ever made to our souls.

"Let us not, however," he adds, "change the Saviour's words. Note carefully He does not say, Whosoever has drunk, but 'drinketh.' He speaks not of one draught, but of the continuous habit of the soul."

XX

ALWAYS ADVANCING

WE HAVE now reached a point in the life of Hudson Taylor, where it becomes so intimately bound up with the history of the China Inland Mission that it is by no means easy to follow the one without the other. But the Story of the Mission has already been told more than once,[1] and unless this volume is to exceed the limits proposed, some new mode of treatment must be adopted for the remaining chapters. Hitherto it has been possible to follow a strictly chronological order, but from this point onward, while not ignoring historical developments, and the main outlines of the Mission's history, events will be grouped in such a way as to bring into prominence the life and influence of the Founder. It is more important to know the mind and character of the man than to follow a bare record of happenings in order of time. The method adopted will, it is hoped, lay emphasis upon his spirit and character, his motives and methods, his ruling ideas and ideals, his principles and practice. At the same time, the main sequence of events will be clearly indicated, and the chronological table, provided in the Appendix, will enable the reader, at a glance, to trace his movements from place to place, and from year to year.

1 *Hudson Taylor and the China Inland Mission: The Growth of a Work of God,* by Dr. and Mrs. Howard Taylor. *The Jubilee Story of the China Inland Mission,* by Marshall Broomhall.

In the autumn of 1871, more than a year after the death of his wife, Hudson Taylor left China for England. He had been deeply mellowed by sorrow and grief, but greatly enriched by a more intimate apprehension of what union and communion with Christ meant. But he had been severely tried by personal sickness, by baneful consequences of the Tientsin massacre, by strenuous efforts of the Chinese Government to restrict missionary liberty, by shortness of funds consequent upon the Franco-Prussian war, and by Mr. Berger's request to be relieved of responsibility for the Home Department of the Mission. Something of what he felt is revealed by the following two sentences, culled from a letter written to his mother during his voyage home:

> "My life work *for* China is far from accomplished, though I am not sure that my work *in* China may not be largely done. One year has been clean lost, and I cannot really and effectively resume it alone."

For five and a half years he had been absent from England, and the necessity for new arrangements to relieve Mr. Berger compelled him to spend the best part of a year at home. On November 28, 1871, he was united in marriage to Miss Faulding, one of the *Lammermuir* party, at the Regent's Park Chapel, the service being conducted by the Rev. Dr. Landels. A home was established at 6 Pyrland Road, London, N., where the Mission's Home centre continued for more than twenty years. But China called, and on October 9, 1872, Mr. and Mrs. Taylor set sail again for China, leaving the work in charge of a newly formed Council, and their children with their trusted friend, Miss Blatchley.

How Hudson Taylor found things on the field may be gauged from the following few words, which at the same time reveal his sane mixture of faith and works: "Though things look very sadly, they are not hopeless; they will look *up*, with God's blessing, if looked after." The next two years were spent in seeking to infuse new life into the work, in visiting all the stations and most of the out-stations, and in striving to develop Chinese workers in the absence of European.

It was during this period that his plans for the evangelization of the whole of China became more clear. He prayed for fifty, or one hundred,

Chinese evangelists for Chekiang alone, and wrote: "I am aiming at claiming no less than every city for Christ." With a view to an advance into Western China he, with Mr. Judd, visited Wuchang, and established a centre there, but the consequences of that journey were far from what he had anticipated. A slip, and a fall, down the steamer's companion-way brought on concussion of the spine, and the gradual development of paralysis of the lower limbs.

It is a striking fact that it was from this time of helplessness that the larger developments of the Mission sprang. It made the word, "For it pleased the Father that *in Christ* should *all* fulness dwell," and not partly in the worker, come home to him with living power. And if any one sentence epitomizes his experiences at this time, it is: "Out of weakness made strong."

When Hudson Taylor reached England in October, 1874, he was threatened with the possibility of never again being able to walk. For many months he was condemned to he on his back, only able, at times, to move himself from side to side by means of a rope fixed over his head. Yet prostrate in his weakness, and unable even to write his own letters, he prayed and planned for developments worthy of God, and in keeping with His commands. With a map of China fixed at the foot of his bed, he proved the power of prayer, and the efficacy of faith in obtaining promises.

It was under these conditions that Hudson Taylor launched his appeal for eighteen men to enter the nine still unoccupied provinces. But it may be well, before we proceed further, to quote a few lines from one of his articles, which gives the key to his aggressive spirit. In a study of Numbers 7, under the title *Princely Service,* he calls special attention to the princes' gift of "six covered wagons, and twelve oxen," for the service of the Tabernacle, and makes this comment:

> "It is interesting to note that the first offerings recorded were for the purpose of assisting in the moving of the tabernacle; it was not God's purpose that it should be stationary."

And then he adds this significant observation:

> "Nor is God's work ever intended to be stationary, but always advancing."

Always advancing was certainly one of the watchwords of Hudson Taylor's life. "Our greatest desire and aim," he wrote in *China's Spiritual Need and Claims,* in 1865, "are to plant the standard of the Cross in the eleven unevangelized provinces of China Proper, and in Chinese Tartary." And now that a substantial beginning had been made, and a base established, the next step came, and that was this appeal for eighteen men. In every way the time seemed inopportune. Hudson Taylor was an invalid, and within a few weeks of the appeal being issued a young Consular officer, Margary, was murdered, and war between Great Britain and China became imminent. But Hudson Taylor wrote:

> "We believe that the time has come for *doing* more fully what He has commanded us; and by His grace we intend to do it. Not to *try;* for we see no Scriptural authority for trying. 'Try' is a word constantly in the mouth of unbelievers.... The word of the Lord in reference to His command is not 'Do your best,' but 'Do it.' We are therefore making arrangements," etc., etc.

What he did not tell the public then, but what may now be told, is that he and Mrs. Taylor had themselves contributed a sum of several thousand pounds towards this forward movement, the greater part of this being from a private legacy left to Mrs. Taylor. They did more than appeal, and more than pray, they sold their all to buy the field. Prayer with them was no shifting of a burden on to God, but a partnership, a working together with God. And the men were given, and while Mrs. Taylor remained at home, Hudson Taylor went out to China with a party of ladies, though the two countries were on the verge of war. Diplomacy had failed so far, "but" wrote Hudson Taylor, "prayer has not failed." And when he and his party landed in Shanghai they learned that the Chefoo Convention had been signed while they were on the sea, and that inland China was thrown open as never before![1]

But before we pass on, we must dwell for a moment upon this consecration of personal wealth, for it casts not a little light upon the character of

---

1　The Treaty of Tientsin, signed in 1858 and ratified in 1860, had theoretically opened China, but this was in part a dead letter until the Chefoo Convention followed.

the man and his wife. Speaking some years later in the Mildmay Conference Hall he gave the following testimony:

> "There was a period in my work when, from bequests and other circumstances, it was left open to myself and to my dear wife, either to live upon the funds which were left us... or to dedicate those funds to His service in other ways. We laid the matter before God. We felt we could not encourage brothers and sisters to go out and simply depend upon Him, if we were accepting, as a better alternative, a living on interests from vested properties.... The conclusion to which we came before God was—it does not affect anyone else—that as His servants it was our privilege to use for His glory whatever He might send, not actually required for our own immediate wants; and we did so, and we have not had cause to regret it. God has proved faithful to us, and is so still. And many of you know, my dear wife and myself do not use any of the general funds of the China Inland Mission."

What the Chefoo Convention meant to the Mission at this time may be gathered from the fact that during the next eighteen months its pioneers travelled more than thirty thousand miles throughout the Empire making known the Gospel.

Shortly before Christmas 1877 Hudson Taylor was home again, glad to be reunited to his wife after a separation of more than a year. On the field he had been guiding the widespread movements of the workers, had taken part in the great Missionary Conference at Shanghai, but had now come home to make more fully known the terrible conditions arising from the famine in China, and to organize more thoroughly the work in England. But though he had been so long separated from Mrs. Taylor, he gladly spared her to go forward to China to engage in famine relief, and especially the care of the orphans. He followed in February, 1879. Though many memorable journeys and important developments belong to this period, such as the opening of work at Chefoo, the visiting of the Kwangsin River, soon to become an important sphere for women's work, we must press on to the autumn of 1881. Again Mr. and Mrs. Taylor separated, Mrs. Taylor going home alone while Mr. Taylor stayed behind and held a memorable conference at Wuchang with a few members of the Mission.

It was a time of unparalleled opportunity, for China was now open and there was urgent need, and immense scope for reinforcements. Possessed and burdened with a sense of great responsibility, it was impressed upon Hudson Taylor's mind to ask for "other Seventy also." Had not God appointed "other Seventy" to assist the twelve in little Palestine? Was it too much to ask Him to do a similar thing for vast and needy China? And the Conference felt the leading to be of God, and not only asked but definitely thanked God, ere they scattered, for the Seventy they knew were coming.

There was really nothing arbitrary in the number chosen. With a sheet of paper before them they had surveyed the field, province by province, and station by station, and the result was this determination to ask God in agreed prayer for forty-two men and twenty-eight women. And in this advance Hudson Taylor practically carried the whole Mission with him, for the appeal was not published until it had been submitted to all the workers, and when it did appear in *China's Millions* it was with no less than seventy-seven autograph signatures.

It was not that funds were plentiful; indeed, for some time the very opposite had been the fact. But, with the resolution to obey, the money came, and in ways that must have brought blessing to many a giver, as well as joy to the heart of God.

In Hudson Taylor the Italian proverb was fulfilled: "He who has love in his heart, has spurs in his side." He was never for taking an easy pace, but ever was for urging God's work forward. With him it was literally, Time versus Eternity. But while he was ever for advancing, he was supremely careful not to go before God. There were several different ways of working for God, he said:

> "We may make the best plans we can, and then carry them out to the best of our ability....
>
> "Or, having carefully laid our plans, and determined to carry them through, we may ask God to help us....
>
> "There is yet another mode of working; to *begin* with God, to ask *His* plans, and to offer ourselves to carry out His purposes."

This distinction was to him all-important, for he could then leave all responsibility with the *Great Designer*. This was the secret of his rest and quiet confidence. It is to be feared we too often forget the deep significance of that familiar prayer:

> "Prevent us, O Lord, in all our doings with Thy most gracious favour, and further us with Thy continual help; that in all our works *begun, continued, and ended in Thee*, we may glorify Thy Holy Name, and finally by Thy mercy obtain everlasting life; through Jesus Christ our Lord."

No sooner had the Seventy sailed, and God's Seventy came to nearly Eighty, than Hudson Taylor set forth for China once more, on January 20, 1885, that he might be in the field to welcome the Cambridge Seven who were to follow in a fortnight. Of the strenuous months which followed, the visiting of at least nine of China's provinces, of the setting apart for the ministry of men like Pastor Hsi, of establishing women's work on the Kwangsin River, of organizing a China Council, arranging for his own deputy in the field, of establishing Training Homes for expected reinforcements, and other far-reaching movements we must not speak. The same belief that God's work must be "always advancing" still urged him on, and with 1886 came another launching out into the deep, for before the close of that year he had cabled home:

> "Banded prayer next year hundred new workers, send soon as possible."

One hundred new workers in one year! Writing of that period of Mission history, Dr. Eugene Stock said: "Does the whole history of Missions afford quite a parallel to

SCRIPTURE TESTIMONY
Ask Me anything in My name
MATTHEW 18:19 · JOHN 14:13-14 · JOHN 16:23-24

this?" Such rapid expansion in a small mission made great demands on all. No fewer than six hundred candidates had to be carefully examined, accommodation had to be enlarged, and funds had of necessity to be increased. But there was at times a touch of humour in Hudson Taylor's references to the serious matter of finance. "There is no fear," he said, "that we shall all have to become vegetarians! for the cattle on a thousand hills, and all the fowls of the mountains are His; and were all the currency of the world insufficient, He has abundance of unmined gold and silver."

How sure he was of God, and that this policy of "always advancing" was His will, is strikingly illustrated by his remarks at the Annual Meetings of the Mission held in London on May 26, 1887, when less than five months of the year, which was to see the hundred sail, had passed.

> "We have the sure word, 'Whatsoever ye shall ask in My Name, I will do it, that the Father may be glorified in the Son.' Resting on this promise, it would not have added to our confidence one whit, if when we began to pray in November, my brother-in-law, Mr. Broomhall, had sent me out a printed list of one hundred accepted candidates. We had been spending some days in fasting and prayer for guidance before the thought was first suggested to our mind. We began the matter aright;—with God—and we are quite sure we shall end aright."

And the close of the year saw all the hundred workers either in China or *en route,* and the income of the Mission had risen 50% to meet the extra demand. To Hudson Taylor the Bible was a *Book of Certainties.* More than once he summed up his own faith, and the basis of the Mission, in these few words:

> "There is a Living God.
> "He has spoken in the Bible.
> "He means what He says, and will do all He has promised."

And so writing about this Book of Certainties he adds:

> "Do we not all need to dwell more frequently on the certainties, the absolute certainty of Divine things? Why is gravitation certain? Because it is a Divine Law. Why is Scripture just as certain? Because it is a Divine Book. Why is prayer offered in the Name of Christ as certain to be answered as the sun to rise? Because both are according to the Divine Will; both are promised in the Divine Scriptures."

There was no daunting a man who believed thus. There were no difficulties which could stay his progress. If laid upon his back in weakness,
he could go down into the valley of humiliation depending upon all the
fulness in Christ, and if he had to face the Hill Difficult, he could do
all things through Christ who strengthened him. He knew the secret of
Pascal's words:

"Do small things as if they were great, because of the majesty of Jesus
Christ, who works them in us, and who lives our life; and great things as
small and easy, because of His omnipotence."

But even the coming of the Hundred did not suggest to him a halt.
It only strengthened faith to ask, and to expect, still greater things, and
from this time dates a wider mission of usefulness which encompassed
the world. But that must be reserved for another chapter. Here we must
still follow his policy of "always advancing."

In October, 1889, Hudson Taylor issued a little pamphlet entitled *To
Every Creature*. After recalling the fact that they were nearing the close of
an important decade in the history of the Mission, he continues:

> "This decade has witnessed the out-going of the eighty mission-
> aries, whom God gave us in response to our prayers for the Seventy,
> and in the following year of forty others, among whom were
> the well-known Cambridge band.... Then we have to praise God
> for the one hundred missionaries given us in 1887, and for the
> more than fifty who followed them last year, including the first
> American party....
>
> "When we turn from the total number of Protestant communi-
> cants—under 40,000—to think of the population of China, the
> contrast is appalling.... The Master's words are 'to every creature;'
> how far are we fulfilling them?...
>
> "How are we going to treat the Lord Jesus Christ in reference to
> this command? Shall we definitely drop the title Lord as applied
> to Him?..."

He then proceeds to indicate how this project could be translated from
proposition into practice, based upon his own experiences as an evangelist

with William Burns. These proposals he submits to the reader for earnest prayer, especially in view of the great Missionary Conference to meet in Shanghai during the following May, when he was to preach the opening sermon.

And when that Conference met this subject was his theme.

> "If as an organized Conference," he said, "we were to set ourselves to obey the command of our Lord to the full, we should have such an outpouring of the Spirit, such a Pentecost as the world has not seen since the Spirit was poured out in Jerusalem. God gives His Spirit not to those who long for Him, not to those who pray for Him, nor to those who desire to be filled always, but He does give His Holy Spirit to them that obey Him."

The idea of an appeal for no less than a thousand new evangelists was earnestly commended to the Conference, and was adopted. And so the call went forth for One Thousand men within the next five years. And when the five years were past Hudson Taylor issued a little booklet to show what God had wrought. One thousand men had been asked for. God's answer had been 481 men and 672 women, or a total of 1153.

We might well bring this chapter to a close at this point. But Hudson Taylor was not satisfied. When peace had been signed between China and Japan in 1895, he urged another advance.

> "An important crisis in China's history has been reached," he wrote. "The war just terminated does not leave her where she stood. It will inevitably lead to a still wider opening of the Empire, and to many new developments.... In view of the new facilities and enlarged claims of China, the next five years should see a larger reinforcement than that called for in 1890."

"A larger reinforcement than that called for in 1890!" And that had been for one thousand men! That there might be spiritual preparation on the field for such further expansion, he approached the Keswick Committee, in regard to the sending of a deputation to China that the spiritual life of the workers might be deepened and strengthened. But just as new workers, who had volunteered, were ready for advance, the Boxer outbreak burst upon the country, and ushered in, by fire and sword, a new era in all missionary undertakings.

By this time, however, Hudson Taylor, though as keen as ever in spirit, was physically unequal to the strain of leadership. But it is significant that when organizing his last advance prior to the Boxer persecutions, he had written:

> "If the Spirit of God works mightily, we may be quite sure the spirit of evil will also be active.... Pray that God will prevent the breaking up of the Empire, and not allow Mission work here to be hindered as it has been in Tahiti, Madagascar, parts of Africa, and elsewhere."

And when the Boxer crisis was over, and the records of the *Martyred Missionaries of the China Inland Mission* were published, he wrote in the Preface to that volume the following words:

> "Will not some hear the voice of the Master calling them to go out and take the place of those called higher.... Let us never forget that a million a month in China are dying without God."

The ruling passion of his life was strong to the very end. He believed in the perpetual need of the wagon and the oxen, that it was not God's purpose that His work should ever be stationary, but Always Advancing.

XXI

THE INCREASE OF GOD

IN THE last chapter we saw something of the ceaseless energy with which Hudson Taylor sought to advance the work of God in China. To that end he laboured day and night, striving according to God's working, which wrought in him mightily. In this chapter we shall see how, somewhat reluctantly at first, he was drawn into a wider ministry than he had anticipated. His prayers were being answered, but in ways he little dreamed of. New and altogether unexpected opportunities were to open out before him in the presence of which he hesitated and even trembled.

From the first, the work he had inaugurated had been on an interdenominational basis, now it was to become international. Such a development inevitably introduced new and complex problems from which he shrank. But "holding fast the Head," as he had done, his influence and ministry were to know an increase which was nothing less than "the increase of God." And so soon as he recognized the hand of God in such increase all fears and hesitations vanished.

He believed in *Blessed Prosperity*. It was the title of one of his helpful Bible studies.

> "There is," he wrote, "a true prosperity which comes from God and leads towards Him.... This divine prosperity is God's purpose for every believer, in *all* that he undertakes; in things temporal,

and in things spiritual, in all the relations and affairs of life, as well as in all work for Christ and for eternity, it is God's will for each child of His that *'Whatsoever he doeth shall prosper.'"*

If this prosperity were not experienced by every child of God he believed there was therein a call for self- examination, for prosperity was promised, and should be claimed. But the conditions must be fulfilled.

"The Word of God," he wrote, "shows clearly that abiding is the condition of fruitfulness, of bearing much fruit, and fruit that shall remain (unlike that blown from the tree ere it ripens and comes to perfection)....

"The distinction between fruit and works is important. Works do not show the character of the worker, but only his skill; a bad man may make a good chair. Works, again, may be good and useful, but do not propagate themselves. Fruit, on the contrary, reveals the character of the fruit-bearer, and has its seed in itself—is reproductive."

This passage is not only an illustration of his powers of exposition, but it is a key to his own life's story, especially to the unsought development of his world-wide ministry. This was fruit for which he had not consciously laboured. And it was unexpectedly abundant, and fruit to abide. Jacob's prophecy concerning Joseph was fulfilled in his case:

> "Joseph is a fruitful bough,
> A fruitful bough by a fountain;
> His branches run over the wall."

In the same year as the Hundred sailed, a pressing invitation arrived in England urging that Hudson Taylor should visit North America. The invitation came first by letter, then by a visit in person of Mr. Henry W. Frost. The support of men like Mr. Moody, Mr. Black- stone, Dr. Pierson, Dr. Gordon, and Dr. Brookes was promised. But Hudson Taylor did not see his way to respond.

"The Lord has given me no light," he said. "I do not think it is His purpose thus to extend the work."

But an independent invitation coming from Mr. Moody, and another from Dr. W. J. Erdman, caused him to reconsider the matter, and at length to promise that he would return to China via America and speak at the Northfield and Niagara Conventions.

On June 23, 1888, therefore, Hudson Taylor, accompanied by his son Howard and Mr. and Mrs. Radcliffe, set sail from Liverpool little knowing what was before them. One tiling they did know, and that was that God's way was perfect.

> "God Himself is at the helm," wrote Hudson Taylor, "ordering all things after the counsel of His own will. He has a plan, and He is carrying it out; He has a throne, and that throne rules over all. Our strength then is to 'sit still,' and look on—it may be with wonder, it may be with awe—but to look on with reverential trust, knowing that 'as for God, His way is perfect.'"

At the Annual Meetings in London, shortly before he sailed, he had said: "God is moving, are we also moving? Are we ready to go on with Him?" He was to find these words more timely than he had imagined, for, of the three months which followed in America it is impossible, in brief space, to give any adequate description. Great and enthusiastic gatherings were held both in the States and in Canada. There was an immense concourse of students at Northfield, and these were deeply impressed by Hudson Taylor's messages. It was the same at Chicago, and at Niagara-on-the-Lake. But still the thought of founding a centre for the China Inland Mission was absent from his mind. But the spontaneity of the giving, and of the consecration, at Niagara brought in a new element which was too manifestly the work of God to be denied. But it was totally unexpected.

> "I had not the most remote idea of our visit to America affecting the China Inland Mission thus," he subsequently wrote. "It was a great surprise, and it led to much prayer that one might know the Lord's purpose in this dealing.... I was very much concerned—I might almost use the word 'frightened.'" And on another occasion he added: "I never felt more timid about anything in my life."

As it is not the purpose of this book to retell the story of the Mission, as already indicated, we must not follow the interesting developments of the work in North America, save as they directly affect Hudson Taylor. In one word it may be recorded that when Hudson Taylor sailed from Vancouver for China in October, 1888, he was accompanied by a band of fourteen North American workers, eight women and six men, the first of many contingents to join the ranks of the Mission from the United States and Canada.

And this enlargement to the work brought a new enlargement into the life of Hudson Taylor.

> "I was quite melted," he wrote, "by the kindness of beloved friends to me.... One felt what a wealth of love and grace there is in the great Church—greater, perhaps, than one had ever conceived before—that after all, all the wide world over, no matter whether in Africa, in India, in China, or in America, in Canada, in Scotland, or in England, all the Lord's children are children of one Father, all bound to one great central heart, and that they are indeed all one in Christ Jesus. It is glorious to realize the Church is one. It is not uniformity that we want, but really manifested heart unity."

It was thus that Hudson Taylor's wider ministry began, a ministry which was to take him to the ends of the earth. In November of the following year, after another visit to North America, to organize this new centre more adequately, and after the publication of the leaflet *To Every Creature* mentioned in the previous chapter, Hudson Taylor, accompanied again by his son Dr. Howard Taylor, responded to some long-standing invitations to visit Sweden and Norway. The kindness and the hospitality he here received exceeded all he had ever known. And the opportunities for service were unbounded. He seldom addressed less than from two to five thousand persons at a time, and some twenty-four towns, in all, were visited. Queen Sophia, at Stockholm, also graciously granted him a private audience, while everywhere the people were drawn to him. "You took me by the heart, and held me there from first to last," said Dr. John Brown to Principal Shairp. And this is what Hudson Taylor did.

It was clear to him now that God was calling other nations to participate in the rapid evangelization of China, and so with the theme of *To Every Creature* in his mind, he wrote:

> "In Scandinavia there are surely one hundred of the thousand additional missionary evangelists needed to carry the Gospel to every family in China."

And in Germany, which country he could not visit then, the reading of his booklet *To Every Creature* kindled such a flame of missionary zeal that jewels, watches, and even wedding rings were placed upon God's altar for His work abroad, leading to the formation of the German China Alliance, one of the associate missions of the China Inland Mission. And the reading of the *Retrospect* by Hudson Taylor, a little later, was used to call into being the Liebenzell Branch of the work also. Thus was the increase of God being given to his ministry in Europe, and through Europe to China.

But this was not all, for while the booklet *To Every Creature* was being penned in England, the hearts of some of God's servants in Australasia were being burdened with the need and claims of China. Hudson Taylor believed that workers were thrust forth in answer to prayer, for had not Christ said: "Pray ye therefore the Lord of the harvest that *He* send forth labourers into His harvest"? And prayer was being answered before ever the appeal was issued, and apart from any mutual conference. The result was, after certain correspondence, the formation of another Home Centre, this time in Australasia, authorized by cable on Hudson Taylor's birthday, May 21, 1890, the day after the conclusion of the Shanghai Conference, when he had preached and appealed for the thousand new workers. And as soon as it was possible he, this time accompanied by Mr. (now Sir) Montagu Beauchamp, set sail for Australia.

Here again, as in North America, the faith and zeal of many Christians were stimulated by personal intercourse with God's servants, and over sixty candidates volunteered for work in China. Of these, eleven were accepted, four from Victoria, three from Tasmania, three from South Australia, and one from New South Wales, and these sailed with Mr. Taylor on November 20, 1890, the first of many contingents from this southern continent.

Auxiliary Councils were then, or subsequently, formed in Sydney, Brisbane, Adelaide, Auckland, and Dunedin. With the Shanghai Conference Appeal fresh in his mind, Hudson Taylor had asked that Australasia might at least send one hundred, and when he visited Australasia the second time, in 1899, this time accompanied by Mrs. Taylor, the last of that hundred passed him on the sea. Thus was the increase of God being given from the southern hemisphere.

There is perhaps no need to follow him in all his several visits to America, to the continent of Europe, and to Australasia. A supernational bond of love was formed in all places he visited, a bond which in the ranks of the China Inland Mission stood the strain of the recent great war without breaking.

He was ever ready to place his experience at the disposal of others, and took long and arduous journeys to serve any of the Lord's people, whether connected with the Mission or not. In 1894 he undertook a long, and to him, perilous journey through the heart of China, in the heat of midsummer, to render service to some workers who were in danger of being withdrawn from the country by their own government, because of methods used unsuited for inland China in those days. And in 1896 he visited India to take counsel with a company of workers on the Indian-Tibetan border, when a critical situation had arisen in regard to their future work.

No one could more heartily enjoy the beauties of God's creation than he, and he revelled in nature's loveliness wherever he went. New Zealand especially impressed him in this respect, and he loved to dwell on God's goodness to him in permitting him to see so much of this world's grandeur in the performance of duties he had not chosen. When he sailed for China in 1853 he had not even contemplated seeing his own country again, all had been surrendered, and now he had seen many of the world's most noted beauty spots. All of this he accepted as the bounty of his Heavenly Father.

In India, in the midst of many engagements, he visited the Black Hole at Calcutta, the Jain and Kali Temples, the Burning Ghat on the banks of the Hoogly, and the sacred city of Benares, and before going on to Darjeeling he made a short pilgrimage to Serampore to see the house, college, and graves of Carey, Marshman, and Ward. The snow-clad peaks of the Himalayas were an almost endless delight, and a visit was paid to Tiger Hill in the hope that he might catch a glimpse of Mount Everest. Whether he saw it or not he did not know!

> "We saw something," he wrote, "either a snow-white cloud where Mount Everest should be seen, or the peak itself: the haze made it impossible to be quite sure. The little trip was very enjoyable and healthful, and we picked some white rhododendrons and orchids in flower."

And these journeys did much to bring relief from the high pressure of office routine which was so often upon him. He had set out in his early days as a young man with China as his only objective, and now, unsought, God had made the world his parish. God had multiplied him exceedingly, and made him as a father to many people of many nations, for in the China Inland Mission alone there were members and associates from between twenty and thirty different countries.

XXII

THE DESIGN OF GOD

WE HAVE considered the urge and drive of Hudson Taylor's spirit, and the widespread influence of his life. In this chapter we desire to look more closely at the character and nature of his work. What were its outstanding characteristics? It had both spirit and form, principles and practice. But to him, just because he was practical, the spirit came first. In all things he knew it was essential to have the mind of God, and to follow the methods and ways of God. God was to him the Great Designer, and he believed that the Scriptures were given that the "man of God may be complete, furnished completely unto every good work." It was in the Scriptures, therefore, that he sought the Design of God in all that pertained to God's work.

Dr. W. A. P. Martin, who knew Hudson Taylor both in his early days and in his later life, speaks of him as becoming "the Loyola of Protestant Missions." And he adds : "When I first met him he was a mystic absorbed in religious dreams, waiting to have his work revealed." But it is impossible to believe that a mere dreamer should become so strong and well-equipped a leader. The true mystic has ever been the most practical of men. In the words of one of our greatest authorities on mysticism, they are those "people who see and experience more vividly a Reality which there is for us all."

173

Believing the words of Christ: "As the Father hath sent Me into the world, even so send I you," Hudson Taylor became an intense student of the Word of God, not only for the nurture of his own spiritual life, but for practical guidance in his life's work. We shall have more to say on this subject elsewhere, but speaking of his work as a leader of men he acted as one who literally believed the words of David:

> "Thy Word is a lamp unto my feet,
>   And light unto my path."

When he wrote that prayer in his Bible at Brighton,

> "Prayed for twenty-four willing, skilful labourers at Brighton, June 25th, 1865,"

he revealed, at the very birth of the Mission, that he had been meditating on God's written Word. "When we first commenced the Mission," he subsequently wrote, "we were encouraged by the promises given to Solomon for the building of the Temple in 1 Chronicles 28:20, 21.

> "Be strong and of good courage, and do it: fear not, nor be dismayed: for the Lord God, even my God, will be with thee; He will not fail thee, nor forsake thee, until thou hast finished all the work for the service of the house of the Lord.
>
> "And, behold, the courses of the priests and the Levites, even they shall be with thee for all the service of the house of God: and there shall be with thee for all manner of workmanship every willing skilful man, for any manner of service: also the princes and all the people will be wholly at thy commandment."

The prayer for willing, skilful workers rings as a refrain right down through Hudson Taylor's life. As he sometimes said: "the willing are not always skilful; and the skilful are not always willing." And in choosing and combining these two words we may be sure that there was much more of that passage in his mind. And what he meant by willing, skilful men must be gathered from his other published writings. Speaking in the Mildmay Conference Hall he said:

"The man who would attempt to build without an architect would not be very wise. But it would be quite as great a mistake to say, because architects are needed, 'We will have none but architects.' And so in missionary effort.... A bricklayer will build better than an architect; and an architect will superintend, and make plans, better than the bricklayer. It is in the combination of 'willing, skilful workers,' suited to every department of service, that the work of God will go on as it ought to do....

"Now, we in the China Inland Mission have asked God for workers of various classes, and He has given them; He has given us men of the highest ability. Most of our English and Scotch Universities, and Trinity College, Dublin, have given us volunteers, and very thankful we have been for them. But we have others who have graduated in different schools....

"I say different advantages, for I hold it to be *sheer infidelity* to doubt that God gives to every one of His children, without exception, those circumstances which are to him the highest educational advantages that he can improve, and which will best fit him for his own work."

There is much more we fain would quote, and the italics are Hudson Taylor's own. The passage illustrates his belief in "the hand of God in every little event of life," and in "a particular providence over each life," to quote his own words again.

But given these willing, skilful men, what was to be their spirit? In answer to this we have an embarrassing wealth of material. In the early editions of *China's Spiritual Need and Claims* no less than ten pages of an appendix are devoted to a consideration of the practical details connected with the "Scriptural principle of becoming all things to all men in order to gain the more."

This related largely to the reasons for adopting the Chinese dress and Chinese mode of life. As some paragraphs of this moving article have been already quoted (see pages 124-5) we must refrain from reproducing more, as we desire to refer to some even more striking articles published during 1885 in *China's Millions*. They are of priceless value, but our quotations must be brief, and selected to illustrate the theme of this chapter: The Design of God.

Under the title *The Secret of Success* the article proceeds to show how, after man's vain struggle for deliverance for four thousand years, "God undertook to save—at His own time, in His own way, by Himself alone, and for His own glory."

> "Well may we ask when and how did He come, and how did He undertake His mighty and glorious task? Did He come when earth's brightest sun was shining with all its noontide splendour, and pale its glories by His own superior effulgence, while the awe-struck nobles of the earth vied with each other in welcoming Him with more than royal honours? No! In the quiet hours of the night, without pomp, and without observation, the Lord of glory stole, as it were, unseen into this sin-stricken world....
>
> "The Wisdom of God, and the Power of God, has undertaken our deliverance, and in order to accomplish it He seeks no alliance with the wisdom, the wealth, the nobility of earth, but *intelligently takes* the lowest place, as that *best adapted* for carrying out His purposes of love and grace....
>
> "Have we learned this lesson? Are we willing to learn it? 'As the Father hath sent Me into the world, even so send I you.' Or are we going to repeat the oft-made experiment— which always has failed, and always must fail—of trying to improve upon God's plan? The poverty and weakness of apostolic missions necessitated reliance on God alone, and issued in wondrous success, and in modern missions it will invariably be found that in proportion to the non-reliance on wealth, or education, or political power, and in proportion to the self-emptying with which they are carried on, the issues are encouraging."

The next article, entitled *Spiritual Science,* is based on the well-known words: "Ye know the grace of our Lord Jesus Christ, that, though He was rich, yet for your sakes He became poor, that ye, through His poverty, might become rich." Of all Hudson Taylor's many Bible expositions we know of none which has so deeply impressed us. Again we must ruthlessly condense.

"Our God is the God of nature as well as of grace; and as He always acts in the *best* way, so, in the same circumstances, He always acts in the *same* way. The uniformity of His mode of action in nature is seen and recognized by many who do not know the great Actor.... But if we speak of the laws of nature, let us not misunderstand the expression. It is the law of a well-regulated household that the door is opened when the door-bell is rung. It would be an entire mistake, however, to suppose that this is *done* by the law: it is done, no matter whether directly or mediately, by the head of the household. So a sparrow 'shall not fall on the ground without your Father.'"

He then proceeds to show that it is *our unchanging God* who makes water boil, or electricity to act. It is *His uniform action* we recognize as the law of gravitation. He then proceeds to the main point of the article *Spiritual Science*.

"No less constant and sovereign is He in the domain of grace: His sovereignty is never erratic or arbitrary. His methods of action may be studied and largely discovered in spiritual things as in natural.... Those who are spiritual have no more difficulty in learning spiritual laws than natural men have in learning natural laws.... Some of the secrets of nature can only be known by the few; but the secrets of grace may be known to *all* the children of God, if they are *willing* to be taught, *and obedient* as they are taught....

"Ten thousand horses could not convey the loads from London to Glasgow in a week that are easily taken in half a day by rail... and so in spiritual things no amount of labour and machinery will accomplish without spiritual power what may be easily accomplished when we place ourselves in the current of God's will, and work by His direction, in His way."

He then speaks of the conditions of success in spiritual things, of God's work done in man's way, and even in the devil's way, which startling statement may be understood by a study of Satan's temptations of our Lord.

> "Would the same sums of money always be contributed if the plate were not passed, or if the donors' names were not published? And yet does any spiritual mind really think that the true work of God is at all advanced by anything done from worldly motives, or to be seen of men? It is a solemn thought that the wood, and hay, and stubble will all be burned up."

Then in closing he shows how the Christ of God saw that the low place, the place of poverty, of weakness, of shame and suffering was the *best* place in which to meet us.

> "In order to enrich us, poor bankrupts, He intelligently and cheerfully emptied Himself of all His riches; and this He did, not by distributing them among us, but by leaving them behind—as neither needed nor suited to effect His purpose. We do well to remember that He was the Wisdom of God and the Power of God, and necessarily chose the *wisest* way and the *mightiest* way to effect His purpose....
>
> "The Corinthian Christians *knew* the grace of our Lord Jesus Christ. Do we? Do we want to know it?... *Are we 'imitators of God'* if we are making no costly sacrifices for the salvation of men? It is our Isaacs who are wanted for the altar, not our superfluity merely. *Are we followers of Christ* if we do not walk in love, as Christ also loved us, and gave Himself up for us?"

Two months later there appeared another article entitled *Lessons from the Incarnation.* The first article had shown how Christ humbled Himself, the second how He emptied Himself.

> "We would fain learn, however, not only what He laid aside— His glory and His wealth—but what He put on, the better to fit Himself for successful ministry; and we are told that the Word was made flesh and dwelt among us.... He stedfastly maintained

his position of being in all things like unto his brethren—a lesson too much forgotten in the prosecution of missionary service."

The application of this is then briefly stated. The missionary naturally leaves his home; he may, or he may not, claim the immunities of his nationality. He may claim the status of a foreigner, or

> "He may assimilate himself in dress, appearance, home, and language to those around him. Nothing is easier than to find objections to this course; but it was the course that Jesus did take, and we are persuaded would still take by us.... It is in this way that, acting for Him, we must show forth the Christ of God.... The Master says, 'I have given you an example that ye should do as I have done to you.... If ye know these things, happy are ye if ye do them.'"

Again, two months later, in an article sent home from China, this same theme is carried one step further by an exposition entitled *Apostolic Example,* based on the words of Paul: "Be ye followers of me, even as I also am of Christ." This may be summed up in the Apostle's own words which are quoted:

> "Though I be free from all men, yet have I made myself servant unto all, that I might win the more.
>
> "And unto the Jews I became as a Jew, that I might win the Jews; to them that are under the law, as under the law, that I might win them that are under the law.
>
> "To them that are without law, as without law (not being without law to God, but under the law to Christ), that I might win them that are without law.
>
> "To the weak I became as weak, that I might win the weak; I became all things to all men, that I might by all means save some. And this I do for the Gospel's sake."

And then Hudson Taylor adds, in summing up this valuable series of articles:

"It is noteworthy that after this remarkable declaration, the Holy Spirit, by the Apostle, exhorts us likewise to 'so run that ye may obtain.' We confidently believe that there is a secret here which would often have spared tried workers the disappointment of years of unsuccessful labour."

We have dwelt at some length on these articles, in which Hudson Taylor laid emphasis upon the mind of God, for they express truths which dominated his life. But he did not search the Scriptures only, to learn the mind of Christ; he meditated long upon them for light upon the right methods of work and organization. The practice as well as the principles upon which he built up the China Inland Mission he found in the Word of God. That Book was to him his *vade-mecum*. The paper entitled the *Principles and Practice of the China Inland Mission* sums up under fifteen heads the definite results of his thinking on these subjects, based upon the experience of many years. It reveals Hudson Taylor as a master builder laying the foundations of the work he had been raised up to establish. His one concern was to find out the mind of God, the design of God, and apply that to the practical problems of the work in China.

This is not the place to consider these in detail. What has been written must suffice to indicate the spirit of the man whose life we are studying. We must conclude this chapter by showing how he found in Scripture justification for widespread itineration as an Evangelizing Agency.

At the Shanghai Conference of 1877 he read a paper on this subject which is still worthy of consideration. It is based on such passages as:

"Jesus went through all the cities and villages, teaching in their synagogues, and preaching the gospel of the kingdom, and healing every sickness and every disease among the people."

Four questions were asked:

1. "What is the necessity for and the actual value of itinerant missionary work? That it is both necessary and of great value might well be assumed from the prominence given to it by our Lord Himself, and also by the Apostles.

...[And] history now proves that the work thus attempted was actually accomplished, and quickly accomplished."

Then follow some exceedingly valuable remarks on the best method of preaching to the Chinese, who are an eminently practical people. After referring to the Word as "incorruptible seed," *i.e.* imperishable seed, he continues:

> "Talk theory to the heathen, and they are generally unmoved; tell them merely of blessings in store for the future, and they are too often sceptical or too occupied with the pressure of present necessities to heed what you have to say. But tell your audience that you have an infallible help for every opium smoker among them, for every drunkard, for every fornicator, for every gambler—that you proclaim a Saviour who has *never once failed* to save immediately any soul that trusted in Him, both from the power of sin and from its eternal consequences, and you will soon see that the Gospel is good news to your hearers, can command attention, and will accomplish the mightiest changes of which the mind of man can conceive, or the heart of man can desire."

2. Under the second head, viz. "What is the place of itinerant work among the various agencies?" Hudson Taylor continued:

> "Here, the Word of God must be our guide, and the example of our Lord and His Apostles, as recorded there, our examples.... Christ sent the Twelve, and the Seventy before His face to every place whither He Himself would come. His own work was but an itinerant and preparatory one—no Church was formed till after Pentecost."

The eminent sanity of Mr. Taylor comes out in this article, for he declines to discuss the *relative* merits of itinerant and localized work.

> "As well might we discuss the relative merits of land and water, of mountain and plain, of animal and vegetable. All exist, all are indispensable; the one does not supersede the other, but supplements it, and is its necessary complement....

"Look on the widespread itinerant work as independent and final, and it fails to meet our expectations. But as a preparatory work it succeeds—always has succeeded, and especially in China, and from *the Design of God,* and the nature of things, it must ever succeed everywhere."

3. The third head deals with the missionary journeys; how best carried on, and what should be attempted. It may be of profit to recall that he laid much stronger emphasis upon preaching than upon colportage.

"Let me repeat—preaching and colportage; not colportage and preaching. I left England for China, nearly twenty- four years ago, believing in colportage. A million Testaments—distribute them! Experience—that of older and wiser men, fully confirmed by my own—taught me that colportage and preaching were *both* needed. Further experience has reversed in my mind the order, and now I would say—preaching and colportage. If you *must* leave either out, let it be the latter. If either must be abridged, let it be the latter, and not the former."

4. On the last point: By whom may such itinerant work be most profitably prosecuted? one brief paragraph must suffice.

"It would only be in very exceptional cases that such work could be undertaken by married missionaries with families. God has other work for them, mark, which they only can do, and plenty of it. As a rule, single young men must commence such work; and they should commence it as soon after their arrival in the field as possible, before their health and strength are too much worn down. The physical strain of months and years spent in such labour is very great."

These quotations will illustrate the way in which Hudson Taylor sought to fashion his work according to the design of God, as revealed in the Scriptures, and from personal and practical experience.

XXIII

THE WORD OF GOD

ORE THAN once, as already recorded, Hudson Taylor stated that his life, and his life's work, were founded upon three facts, namely, that:

"There is a Living God.
"He has spoken in the Bible.
"He means what He says, and will do all He has promised."

Since the Word of God occupied so fundamental a place in his life, it is essential that a chapter should be devoted to this subject. There can be no understanding of the man otherwise. And in this matter as in others, it is best to let him speak for himself. The opinions of a man who has staked a long and successful career in dependence upon any truth necessarily commands attention. Academic questions concerning the inspiration of the Bible may be discussed indefinitely, but practical experience becomes an unanswerable argument. A former Headmaster of Rugby has well said:

"I feel most strongly that the real way to test the inspiration of the Bible, or any other book, is not by criticizing its text, but by watching its influence upon human lives. In that, after all, we have definite and distinct evidence of its miraculous and supernatural character."

Toward the end of his full life, after he had seen sail more than five hundred men and women, who "were willing to prove their faith by going into inland China with only the guarantees they carried within the covers of their pocket Bibles," Hudson Taylor said:

"The living God still lives, and the living Word is a living Word, and we may depend upon it; we may hang upon any word that God ever spoke, or ever caused by His Holy Spirit to be written. Forty years ago I believed in the verbal inspiration of the Scriptures. I have proved them for forty years and my belief is stronger now than it was then. I have put the promises to the test. I have been compelled to do so, and I have found them true and trustworthy.

"We want to impress upon you that the Word of God is God's own Word. If I did not believe in the inspiration of a Bank of England note, if I was not quite sure whether the note that professed to be for £50 would be cashed for £5 or £50, it would not be worth very much to me.... What would you have thought if I had been foolish enough—nay, I might say dishonest enough— to part with it for less than it represented? I wish that I could say that I have been as faithful to the Word of God. Oh, how often I have discounted God's promise and been surprised, almost, at getting a small part of that promise fulfilled, instead of expecting and claiming all.

"But we can tell you something more than this. We have found that when our faith has broken down, even in God's own Word, His faithfulness has not broken down, and that when we have been poor children, we have had a very kind Father, that when we have been unworthy servants, we have had a glorious Master. 'If we believe not, yet He abideth faithful. He cannot deny Himself.'"

There is much more that could be quoted of a like and supplementary effect, such as, for instance, the importance of not only grasping the general purport of Scripture, but of seeking out the particular meaning of each important word. Hudson Taylor was both a comprehensive and an intensive student of the Bible. He was both thorough and methodical, as will be seen by a consideration of his method of reading that "Book of Certainties," as he called it.

From his youth he had been taught to read the Bible systematically, and concerning his own plan he wrote in later years as follows:

"We would earnestly advise the consecutive reading of the whole Word of God to all who do not so read it; and to all who are able to do so, that the whole Bible be read over in the course of the year; but where this cannot be done prayerfully and thoughtfully, rather let a shorter portion be taken for daily reading, still going through the whole of the Word consecutively.

"The plan of reading is comparatively unimportant. A very simple one was pointed out to us many years ago, namely, that Bagster's Bible, exclusive of the Psalms, contains a leaf, or four columns for every day of the year. The New Testament is one-fourth of the Bible, so that an average reading of three columns of the Old Testament, and one of the New each day, will carry one through by the end of the year. There are also eighty-eight columns of the Psalms, and ninety-one days in a quarter, so that a daily average reading of rather less than a column will allow us to go through the Psalms four times in a year.

"It will be noted that we have mentioned that an average reading of so much of the Old, or New Testament, or the Psalms, as the case may be, will suffice; for, of course, no intelligent reader would stop at the end of a column irrespective of the subject matter, but would read to-day a little more and to-morrow a little less, as the subject might call for. And again, some portions would be found so full of meditation as to necessitate a shorter reading, to be made up for at another time.

"We have ourselves used this method for more than thirty years with great profit, though it has often necessitated rising before daylight in order to accomplish it."

This habit of early rising for Bible reading and prayer calls to mind one of his aphorisms which would make an admirable watchword for any Bible-reading association. It reads:

"Do not have your concert *first,* and then tune your instrument *afterwards.* Begin the day with the Word of God and prayer, and get first of all into harmony with Him."

One of his little books, running to one hundred and twenty pages, owed its message and publication to this habit of consecutive reading. It is entitled *Separation and Service,* being a study of the, humanly speaking, uninteresting chapters, Numbers 6 and 7. He was on a missionary journey and was compelled to spend the night in a particularly wicked town. All the inns were places to abhor, and the people seemed to have seared consciences. His own heart was oppressed, and he awoke in the morning much cast down, and feeling spiritually hungry and thirsty.

"On opening my Bible," he subsequently testified, "at the seventh chapter of Numbers, I felt as though I could not then read that long chapter of repetitions; that I must turn to some chapter which would feed my soul. And yet I was not happy in leaving my regular portion; so after a little conflict I resolved to read it, praying to God to bless me, even through Numbers vii. I fear there was not much faith in the prayer; but oh! how abundantly it was answered, and what a feast God gave me! He revealed to me His own great heart of love, and gave me the key to understand this and the previous chapter as never before."

At the close of that little book, long since out of print, he says, "May God make our meditation very practical." This was one feature that characterized all his Bible studies—they must be practical.

"Why is so much time worse than wasted," he said, "over criticism of different books? What is needed is the humble, prayerful meditation of those who are determined to do the will of God."

It was the blessedness of literally obeying the Scriptures upon which he laid such emphasis.

"The words, 'the Law of the Lord,' which we understand to mean the whole Word of God, are very suggestive," he wrote. "They indicate that the Bible is intended to teach us what God would have us *to do;* that we should not merely seek for the promises, and try to get all we can from God; but should much more earnestly desire to know what He wants us *to be* and *to do* for Him.

"It is recorded of Ezra, that he prepared his heart to seek the Law of the Lord, in order that he might *do* it, and *teach* in Israel statutes and judgments. The result was that the hand of his God was upon him for good, the desires of his heart were largely granted, and he became the channel of blessing to his whole people."

His expositions of Scripture always came down to the bed-rock of obedience, of some practical issue. "If ye know these things, happy are ye if ye do them." He was no doctrinaire. As a teacher, and as a preacher, his strength lay in the practical application of truth. Speaking, for instance, at the close of one of the Mildmay Conferences when the subject was "The Knowledge of God," he opened his remarks as follows:

"We have been considering together for the last three days the subject of the Knowledge of God.... And now comes the responsibility. We are going away. Where are we going? What are we going to do? How are we going to live? How are we going to serve this gracious One, the knowledge of Whom has been our theme from day to day?

"The practical part of our subject... is very closely connected with the meditations of the preceding days. There is a far closer connection than we sometimes realize between the knowledge of God and practical use of that knowledge.... We cannot separate these things.... We only know that through which we have passed...."

He then proceeded to give a vivid picture of what it cost his mother to say good-bye to him when he first set sail for China. And what a power he had to bare his heart, and speak of the most intimate things of the spirit!

> SCRIPTURE TESTIMONY
>
> *For God so loved the world that He gave His only Son*
>
> JOHN 3:16

"I shall never forget the cry of anguish that was wrung from that Mother's heart as she felt that I was gone. It went to my heart like a knife. I never knew so fully as then what 'God so loved the world' meant; and I am quite sure that my precious Mother learned more of the love of God for the world in that hour than in all her life before.

"Oh, friends! when we are brought into the position of having practical fellowship with God in trial, and sorrow, and suffering, we learn a lesson that is not to be learnt amid the ease and comfort of ordinary life. This is why God so often brings us through trying experiences."

He then, as a further illustration, told a little of what his first-born child Gracie had been to him, and how she had been taken from them, and then added:

"As I stood over her grave, I thanked God that it was in His service, and for China, that He called me to part with my loved child. I knew then, still more fully than before, what 'God *so* loved the world' meant.

"That is how some of us have been led on in the knowledge of God. He has given us to have sympathy with Himself, in His not withholding His only begotten Son, and in that Son giving Himself in order that the world might be saved....

"It will not suffice to sing,

'Waft, waft, ye winds, the story.'

"No! mothers must give up beloved sons; fathers must give up precious daughters; brothers and sisters must cheerfully yield one another to the Lord's service in China, and Africa, and India.... It is in the path of obedience and self- denying service that God reveals Himself most intimately to His children. Would that I could give you an idea of the way in which God has revealed Himself to me in China, and to others whom I have known. In the presence of bereavement, in the deepest sorrows of life, He has so drawn near to me that I have said to myself, Is it possible that the precious one who is in His presence can have more of the presence of God than I have? Is it possible that more manifestation of Himself *can* be given there than here?"

In addition to this practical note which was so characteristic of his addresses, he possessed a powerfully lucid way of so presenting truth that his expositions were easily remembered. One or two previously unpublished illustrations of this may be given.

Speaking on the words, "Oh magnify the Lord with me!" he asked the question:

> "How can we magnify God who is so great? We cannot make Him greater. No; but when we use a pair of binoculars or a telescope to look, say, at the moon, we do not expect to make the moon any bigger than it is, but to bring it nearer. And when we magnify God, we do not make Him greater, but we bring Him nearer to thousands from whom He seems very far off."

Or again, when speaking at family prayers at Shanghai, one Christmas morning, on the familiar words, "Unto you is born this day in the city of David a Saviour, which is Christ the Lord," he turned to the children and said:

> "When, one day, father told you that a little brother had been born to you, you did not make him your brother, he was born your brother. You may have been glad or sorry, you may have welcomed him or not, but he was still born your brother. And Jesus Christ has been born to you a Saviour. You do not make Him such. But you have power to welcome Him as such, if you will, or to reject Him."

Expositions such as these, so simple in one sense, and yet so helpful, are not easily forgotten. They were unique and inimitable. What he aimed at was, that God's Word and truth might not be "matters of mere creed or head-knowledge, but part and parcel of our spiritual and mental being."

"When will it dawn on the Lord's people," he said in a letter to a friend, "that His command to preach the Gospel to every creature was not intended for the waste-paper basket?" The Bible was for him literally true, and to be literally obeyed.

XXIV

THE MAN HIMSELF

I N THE preceding pages some of the outstanding features of Hudson Taylor's personality have been either directly indicated or, at least, suggested. In this chapter an attempt will be made to outline other important elements in his character to which little or no reference has been made.

We are tempted to begin by speaking of his largeness of heart, for this was one of his prominent characteristics, but that will perhaps be the better appreciated if attention first be directed to his great work as "God's Fingerpost"—to use one of his own phrases —directing men and women to China.

As a young man of twenty, we find Hudson Taylor writing to his mother: "I feel as if I could not live if something is not done for China." The evangelization of China was his

SCRIPTURE TESTIMONY
Spiritual burden for a lost people group to be saved
ROMANS 9:1-3

burden, the passion of his life, and all his energies were concentrated to that end. It is said of Cato, that he closed every speech, no matter what its subject might be, with the words, "Carthage must be destroyed;" and, with an infinitely higher aim, Hudson Taylor could not speak without including an appeal for the evangelization of China. Few men knew better how to present the facts, how to press them home, and how to touch the heart with their significance. Maps, charts, tables, illustrations, incidents, with their pathetic appeal, all had their place. "Missionary intelligence is essential to missionary effort," he wrote. "And the more definite the information the better." And he showed great art, and unwearied persistence, in driving these truths home.

> "You will not be wearied," he once said, "by my reiteration of the oft-told fact which may not be, *must* not be forgotten. More than half China Proper is still destitute of one resident Protestant Missionary. All Tibet, and nearly all Mongolia and Manchuria are as totally neglected. Many Roman Catholic missionaries from Europe are labouring in these regions (above one hundred), while we, who owe so much to God, are doing nothing for them. This should not be; this must not continue."

On another occasion he wrote again:

> "How long shall this state of things be allowed to continue? We asked this question in the first edition of our pamphlet on *China's Spiritual Need and Claims,* issued twelve years ago; we have asked it in each successive edition; we ask it still.... What is your reply?"

He never wearied of arraying the facts before the Christian public, and of getting to close quarters with his hearers, or readers, in their application. He knew how to appeal to the imagination, how to speak to the conscience, and how to move the heart also. He could be intensely personal. Quoting those words which had had such a powerful effect upon his own life, "If thou forbear to deliver them that are drawn unto death," he would proceed:

> "These words are the words of God; very simple, very unmistakable, and very solemn. They are addressed, Christian reader, to you. Not to you *alone,* yet to you in *particular;* and you alone must bear your own burden, in respect of them, when you stand before the judgment seat of Christ."

He himself was so dominated by creative convictions that he could make them contagious. Few stories could he tell with more profound impression than that of the drowning of a Chinese fellow-passenger, called Peter, which took place before his eyes in 1856. Space will not permit the full account, as given in *China's Spiritual Need and Claims*, to be reprinted; only a summary from one of his articles, entitled *Individual Responsibility*, is possible, with its pointed application:

> "A Chinaman fell into the river. Numbers of Chinese saw it from the shore; but it was not *their* business; they did not attempt the rescue, though they might have effected it. Others were in boats not far off, and might have rendered help; but *they* were all right; as to the drowning man, that was his look out. So it proved: he was drowned; but *who was responsible for his death?* He who created the law of gravitation? or those who left him to perish? Members of Christian Churches, we have rejoiced that *we* were all right; as for the people of Chinese Tibet, we have left them to their fate. They *have* perished while we were rejoicing: but is this the spirit of Christ? 'He that withholdeth corn, the people shall curse him.'"

But a large measure of his power of appeal lay, not in the facts alone, but in his own impressive personality. He had a way, not given to every man, of baring his own heart. He could speak with freedom of the most intimate experiences, of his trials and sorrows, his bereavements and anxieties, his times of want and times of deliverance, of his spiritual failures and spiritual triumphs in Christ. He took his hearers by the heart, he admitted his readers into his most sacred confidences, and men were drawn to him, and knit to him, in the deepest things. This is apparent on almost every page of *A Retrospect,* and on many a page of *China's Millions* when he was editor. There are few, for instance, who could speak helpfully in the following intimate manner on the words, "He will rest in His love."

> "Before I left China last time this passage was made very precious to me. But it wasn't till I got to Paris that I learned the full preciousness of this clause. There I was met by my beloved wife, and as we sat in the cab side by side, though she had so much to say, and I had too, I could only take her hand and be

silent. The joy was so unspeakable; and oh, it came to me, if all this earthly affection is only a type, what must it be when He is 'silent in His love.'"

Few things did more, in the early days of the Mission, to build up a body of friends and donors than the tone and touch of his correspondence. One or two quotations will be the best illustration of this. Writing of the deepening of spiritual sympathy and loving interest on the part of donors, he gave in *China's Millions* some specimens. One or two of these we quote, with his comments.

SCRIPTURE TESTIMONY
Giving all one has to live on, and trusting God for provision
MARK 12:41-44 · LUKE 21:1-4

"When you were in —," wrote one friend in Scotland, "I heard you pleading for China, and you asked us to look at home if there was anything we could give to forward the cause of God. Well, I cannot at present send money, but *I have looked,* and found the lace Maltese shawl—the gift of my dear husband, now gone Home—which I will post at the same time as this note, and which I hope you will accept for the cause so dear to your heart."

"Need we say," wrote Hudson Taylor, "that our eyes filled with tears—tears of joy—as we felt that Jesus stood first in that loving heart? And we thought of the gladness of His heart at that gift, so inexpressibly precious to the giver —aye, and so inexpressibly precious to the true Receiver, the Lord Jesus Christ."

Judging by this comment—and the few words quoted above are only part of what he said—the reader will believe that the letter acknowledging such a gift would be full of rich appreciation. Then comes another letter, enclosing 5s., asking that this small sum be accepted for the work.

"We did not think the sum small," wrote Hudson Taylor. "Multiplied by all the love it represented, and by all the prayers that accompanied it, we feel it to be a priceless gift, and are gladdened and encouraged by it."

Then came another letter, with a name which could not fail to touch a tender chord in his heart. It was written in a large childish hand, and addressed from an English University town.

> "DEAR SIR—I want to help the boys and girls of China to love Jesus, as it says in *The Children's Treasury* for 1876. I have just been reading about it. If you have not died since then, I want you to let me know; and I will send you a little money I have saved. Your affectionate,
>
> GRACIE —."

Concerning this epistle, signed with the name of his own beloved first-born child, now dead, he wrote:

> "Our reply to this sweet little letter, that cheered and encouraged our hearts not a little in the toil of His loving service, was soon followed by another, from our dear young friend."

This was as follows:

> "DEAR SIR—My father says I may send *all my money* if I like, so I have drawn it out of the Post Office Savings Bank—four shillings—so I now send it, and hope it will help to make the little boys and girls in China good and happy."

How we should like to see his acknowledgment of this dear child's gift! About the same time came another letter, enclosing twenty shillings from an old man in his 90th year. Commenting on both their letters together, Hudson Taylor wrote:

> "Our hearts could not but sing a song of praise as we saw Him leading little Gracie, and our valued old friend in his ripe old age, to sympathize with and aid the same objects according to their means."

Such letters were, as he said, "as a very box of alabaster, broken at the feet of our Lord, whose fragrance filled our heart, as well as rejoiced His." His own heartfelt appreciation, and the personal touch in all his letters acknowledging such gifts, could hardly fail to knit donor and receiver together in a common fellowship for China.

"Are we not partners in this blessed, most blessed service?" he wrote to the friends at home in a letter from the heart of China. "You supply by your sympathy, and prayers, and contributions, our lack; and we who are here seek to make up for your personal inability to preach Christ among the Chinese."

It will have been seen that it was much more than the gifts themselves which moved his heart. With the Apostle Paul he could say: "Not that I seek for the gift; but I seek for the fruit that increaseth to your account." It is therefore no great transition in thought to pass from this devotion to China to his largeness of heart towards all God's people, and all God's work.

"When you are praying for China," he wrote, "always bear in mind what a God He is to whom we are drawing near. China is not a great thing for Him, though it is a great thing for us. Let us bear in mind that His love is as great to India and Africa, and all parts of the world, as to China. Let us seek to cultivate largeness of heart; it will be a blessing to our own souls, and it will bring us into deeper sympathy with God."

> SCRIPTURE TESTIMONY
>
> *Body of Christ is made up*
> *of many members*
>
> I CORINTHIANS 12:12-31

This was the spirit he ever cultivated himself. Though deeply engrossed in his own work for China, and bearing heavy responsibilities, he rejoiced in the prosperity of every organization for the spread of the Gospel. This was manifest in many ways. In the columns of *China's Millions* he published comprehensive surveys of what was being done by all Protestant Missionary Societies in China, and he devoted also considerable space to the work of individual missions. It was not an uncommon thing to set apart a whole page every month to the work of some other Society, taking them *seriatim*. At times, practically a whole number was reserved—twelve pages out of sixteen, for instance, in 1877—for a report of some important Missionary Conference.

"We can only cry to God," he wrote, "to incline His people to strengthen every Protestant Mission; and for ourselves our prayer now is, that the Lord will double our numbers, and increase our usefulness tenfold."

Or again:

"I do not mind what Society they go out under, if they will only go."

Speaking at the Annual Meetings of the Mission in London one year, he said:

"Much has naturally been said at these meetings about the China Inland Mission, but I should not like them to close without an expression of our gratitude to God for His blessing on the work of all the other Protestant Missions in China.... Our work is not in rivalry with any other, it is *sui generis*, and auxiliary, and supplementary. We can therefore rejoice, and we do rejoice, in the success of any who are carrying the Gospel to that needy land."

When he was preaching the opening sermon of the great Missionary Conference in Shanghai, in May 1890, he alluded to the fact that the British and Foreign Bible Society was holding its Annual Meetings in Exeter Hall, London, on the same day, and before he commenced his discourse prayed specially for the Bible Society, and for all other Annual Meetings being held at that season. It was a characteristic act.

"I am quite sure," he said, in the course of that sermon, "we cannot obey the command of God with regard to China, and yet any other country be left unblessed. For the field is the whole world, and the heart of God is so large that no part of the world is outside His thought."

As he had refused, in his paper read before the 1877 Conference, to discuss the relative value of itinerant and localized missionary work, any more than he would discuss the relative merits of land and water, mountain and plain, so now in his sermon he could say:

"The great Commission which our Master has given us is
expressed in several different ways.... The different wordings...
are all to be considered, the plans of service that He leads us to
adopt are to be diverse in their methods and kinds, and very
inclusive.

"I do not know of any kind of missionary work in China, and
I have never heard of any, on which the Lord's blessing has not
rested, or cannot rest, and in which we may not hope to see great
enlargement."

Only a generous-minded, large-hearted man could have spoken thus,
especially when he felt called to emphasize widespread evangelism. Though
he knew that there were those who criticized his line of work, he would
not, and he did not, criticize others. He had no desire to stand aloof, but
rejoiced in fellowship and cooperation.

> SCRIPTURE TESTIMONY
>
> *As Jesus and the Father are one,*
> *so is His desire for all believers*
>
> JOHN 17:11 ·
> JOHN 17:21-23 · ROMANS 15:5-6

"Our blessed Lord," he
said, "fully realized His
oneness with His disciples
and their oneness with
Him. He would do noth-
ing independently of them,
and I think there is a lesson for us to learn, that we should not
work independently of one another. If our Lord worked through
His disciples, and would not work independently, how closely
should we be knit together, and with what practical co-operative
oneness do the work He has given us to do."

It was not that he wholly agreed with all that others did or said. He could
agree to differ, and yet continue fellowship. In his early days in China, he
and William Burns did not see eye to eye on the great subject of our Lord's
return, but they had such heart-to-heart fellowship that they said one to
another "You look for it in one way and I look for it in another, but we
both look for the same Lord; so we can go on together." Concerning the
1877 Conference he wrote:

"Though diverse views were freely and faithfully expressed, a spirit of harmony and brotherly love prevailed."

At the 1890 Conference he had reason strongly to dissent from one of the speakers, and carried the Conference with him in his protest; but one of the last photographs ever taken of him was in company with the one from whom he had differed—a tribute to both men.

Not far removed from this catholicity of spirit was what we may call his common-sense, or balance. Though he will ever be remembered as a man of faith, he was not less a man of works. Trust in God was never for him an excuse for neglect of wise precautions. It was rather a partnership with God which called for the most strenuous effort. No man was more methodical and thorough. And if the parentage of the word "common-sense" is, as Archbishop Trench says, "the common judgment of well-balanced natural senses," Hudson Taylor was a well-balanced man. He saw the dangers of excess, and though full of zeal was never a zealot. "Things will soon look up, with God's blessing, if looked after," well expressed his views.

When preaching before the Shanghai Conference on the miracle of the loaves and fishes, and while urging the Conference to a great venture of faith, he added:

"To return, the miracle was wrought methodically. The disciples were not told to act in any erratic or fanatical way, but the common-sense that God had given them was to be used. Our Saviour Himself methodized His arrangements, and gave them the work to do in a way in which it was possible speedily and satisfactorily to accomplish it."

His appeal at this time was for "intelligent obedience." Another aspect of his sagacity was his anxiety to appear always loyal to the Chinese Government.

"The fact that there is so much to deplore," he wrote in a letter to the friends of the Mission, "must not lead us to forget that there is also much—very much—to commend. Under the providence

of God we enjoy a large measure of peace and safety, protection
and facility for the prosecution of our work through the rule of
the present dynasty.... It will only help us for it to be known that
true Christians are loyal, and seek the good of those that rule
China, as well as of the governed."

Without being dilettante, Hudson Taylor was exact and precise in the
smallest details, as well as in the larger issues. This was specially noticeable
in his handwriting up to the end. And this arose from his sense of responsibility to God in all things, the least as well as the greatest. No one can
understand his character if this be overlooked.

"Should not the little things of our daily life," he wrote, "be
as relatively perfect in the case of each Christian as the lesser
creations of God [a butterfly's wing] are absolutely perfect.
Ought we not to glorify God in the formation of each letter
that we write, and as Christians to write a more legible hand
than unconverted people can be expected to do? Ought we
not to be more thorough in our service, not simply doing well
that which will be seen and noticed, but as our Father makes
many a flower to bloom unseen in the lonely desert, so to do
all that we can do, as under His eye, though no other eye ever
take note of it?

"It is our privilege to take our rest and recreation for the
purpose of pleasing Him; to lay aside our garments at night
neatly (for He is in the room, and watches over us while we
sleep), to wash, to dress, to smooth the hair, with His eye in
view; and, in short, in all that we are, and in all that we do, to
use the full measure of ability which God has given us to the
glory of His Holy Name."

In reading these words we almost seem again to see Mr. Taylor busy
over something, yet at leisure; in labours more abundant, yet "calm on
tumult's busy wheel." His words, "as our Father makes many a flower to
bloom unseen in the lonely desert," recalls an incident in Switzerland after
ill-health had compelled him to lay his burden down.

Climbing one afternoon up a wooded hill-side, we came across some flowers blooming in that secluded spot. Pausing and gazing at them, he quoted the well-known lines of Gray:

> "Full many a gem of purest ray serene
> The dark unfathom'd caves of ocean bear:
> Full many a flower is born to blush unseen,
> And waste its sweetness on the desert air."

Then in his own quiet way he added: "As though a thing were wasted simply because man had not seen it, when the Creator Himself delighteth in all His own handiwork! How easily we forget God!" It was one of those little incidental remarks which revealed how he lived in all things in the presence of God. His belief that God was watching over and delighting in even that hidden flower was the secret of his rest and trust, of his quietness and confidence.

XXV

PIONEER AND BUILDER

ALTHOUGH WE have not followed the latter portion of Hudson Taylor's life in chronological sequence, the reader will have recognized that he was essentially a pioneer, and a pioneer in more senses than one. He was always seeking to break new ground, always keen to enter unoccupied territory, always anxious to proclaim the Joyful News where Christ had not been named. But he was equally a pioneer in his methods, in his return to apostolic precedents; in trusting God, and God alone, for men and for supplies; in taking God, with a daring faith, at His word. He was also a pioneer in missionary organization, and in preferring the direction of the work on the field itself, rather than from home. Ordinarily, the headquarters of a Mission are at home, and the work in many lands. With him the work was in one field, and the home departments in many countries.

But he was more than a pioneer; he was a builder. This fact stands out in bold relief if we contrast his work with that of Gutzlaff. It is an interesting coincidence that Hudson Taylor was born when Gutzlaff was engaged in his daring voyages up and down the China coast. Gutzlaff was a pioneer of a remarkable order, a man of great enterprise, of burning zeal, and amazing industry. His passionate ardour powerfully influenced Hudson Taylor's early enthusiasm, and brought into being the Chinese Evangelization

Society which sent him to China. But Gutzlaff, though Hudson Taylor called him the grandfather of the China Inland Mission, was no builder. He could, and did, profoundly stimulate others, but his own attempts at organization signally failed. But in Hudson Taylor, God combined in a re-markable degree the daring of the innovator with the constructive gifts of the statesman. He was bold without being rash, eager but vigilant, confident but prudent, venturesome but yet far-sighted.

The man who dares to violate custom, to break through precedents, to brave the censure of the world, must also possess strong creative faculties, or he may seem a mere fanatic. It demands rare courage to do what no one else has done before, but it needs courage mixed with prudence, or enthusiasm may run riot. Hudson Taylor possessed both qualities. He did not fear to be peculiar. Writing on the implicit obedience demanded of the Nazarite, he said:

> "God claims the right to determine the personal appearance of His servants.... To many minds there is the greatest shrinking from appearing peculiar; but God would often have His people unmistakably peculiar.... While we are not to seek to be peculiar for its own sake, we are not to hesitate to be so when duty to God renders it necessary, or when the privilege of self-denial for the benefit of others calls for it."

And so we find him as a pioneer adopting Chinese dress, conforming to Chinese customs and modes of life, travelling native fare, encouraging single women to live in the interior of China, refusing to appeal for funds, establishing schools for missionaries' children in the field instead of at home, developing business departments within the Mission to facilitate the supply of temporal needs, building interdenominationally and internationally, and in other ways departing from precedents.

Without entering into any detailed exposition of these more or less original features of his work, which might interest the administrator but not the general reader, it will be sufficiently evident that in Hudson Taylor there were fused bold initiative and daring originality with equally striking constructive ability. He was a pioneer who knew how to build. Ideals were realized, visions materialized, promises were obtained, prayers were answered, and confidences were justified.

Looking back over his long life, Hudson Taylor could say, at the close of his ministry:

> "I have sometimes met people who have said: 'trusting God is a beautiful theory, but it won't work.' But praise God, it has worked, and it does work. I remember a dear friend, an aged minister in London, who said to me in the year 1866 [when the *Lammermuir* party sailed]: 'Well, you are making a great mistake in going to China with no organization behind you. We live in a busy world, and you will be all forgotten, and the Mission won't live seven years.' That was the prophecy of this good man—a wise man too. But he was mistaken; and I could only say to him in a very simple way: 'I have got four children. I have never yet needed a committee to remind me of their needs or of my duty to them; and I do not think I have more care for my children than my Heavenly Father has for His children, whom He is thrusting out into China.'
>
> "Well He has cared for them through all these years, and He has graciously helped us; and, as the work grew, He has given the organization which we had no need for, and no place for, at the commencement. But the organization has grown up with the work."

Here we see the simple-hearted, trustful pioneer not despising organization, nor impatient with method, but ready for both, as time and circumstances demanded. In him the heroic element was well balanced with sagacity and foresight. He had a keen sense of the perils of emotionalism, and on one occasion said in public:

> "We do so much want your prayers, beloved friends, that the Lord will keep us from unwisdom, and from doing anything that might be a cause for subsequent regret and difficulty. If the Spirit of the Lord does indeed guide us, surely He will make us prudent. David was prudent, because the Spirit of the Lord guided him in his movements. So we do ask your prayers that in all that is done in connection with the Mission a spirit of prudence may prevail."

The casual observer is naturally more impressed by the sensational elements in the Mission's history—such, for instance, as the going forth of one hundred new workers in one year—but those who know the inner history know something of the prayer, the deliberations, the careful preparations which preceded and accompanied such developments. The following extract from an address given at the New York Ecumenical Missionary Conference in 1900—one of his last public utterances—will give one a glimpse into the less public side of his life:

SCRIPTURE TESTIMONY
Believers praying together for many days
ACTS 1:14

"It is not lost time to wait upon God," he said. "May I refer to a small gathering of about a dozen men in which I was permitted to take part, some years ago, in November 1886? We, in the China Inland Mission, were feeling greatly the need of Divine guidance in the matter of organization in the field, and in the matter of reinforcements, and we came together before our conference to spend eight days in united waiting upon God—four alternate days being days of fasting as well as prayer."

There is no need to prolong the quotation. It must suffice to say that this Conference saw both the birth and formation of the China Council of the Mission for better organization on the field, and, at the same time, the sending forth of the call for one hundred new workers during the following year, 1887. Those eight days of prayer, with alternate days of fasting, were what Hudson Taylor called "beginning right with God." And so sure was he of God's guiding hand, that he could add:

"We had a thanksgiving, for the men and the money that were coming, in November 1886, and they were all received and sent forth before the end of December 1887."

But we must now take up the story of the closing years of this strenuous career. In the 'nineties, after more than thirty years of leadership of a rapidly growing and expanding work, it began to be evident that his powers of mind and body were unequal to the heavy and constant strain of such responsibilities. The signs of an apostle had been wrought in his life. He had been in labours abundant, in fastings, and in watchings. He had once confessed that "the sun had never risen upon China without finding me at prayer." In his serving the Lord he had been both fervent in spirit and diligent in business. Half-hearted he could not be. The spirit in which he laboured is revealed in the following words of his:

> "Self-denial surely means something far greater than some slight and insignificant lessening of our self-indulgences!"

What self-denial meant to him in just one department of his life, *i.e.* separation from wife and children, is brought home by the following statement, made at the New York conference, on the marriage of missionaries:

> "I do not know any more difficult question in the whole mission-ary problem. I have had the pleasure of living as a married mission-ary for forty years, and I know all the advantages, and the comfort, and the blessings to the work of having a faithful and competent partner by one's side; but for nearly twenty years of my married life, my wife has had to be in one part of the world while I have been in another."

How changeful his lot was may be gauged from the fact that of the nearly fifty-two years from his first sailing to China in 1853 to his death in 1905, almost exactly twenty-seven years were lived in China, while the remaining twenty-five years were spent in other lands, or on the sea. As he travelled to China, from England alone, no less than eleven times, his early journeys being by sailing ship, he had a fairly full opportunity of knowing something of God's mighty wonders in the deep. Of his thirty-five years of active leadership of the China Inland Mission, from its inception in 1865 up to his breakdown in 1900, a little over twenty of these years were spent in China itself, and the remaining fifteen years in one or other of the home countries, organizing and developing the work, or travelling to and fro. These facts show what a roving life he led, and how little he can have known of the joys and comforts of a home.

A reference to the movements of Hudson Taylor during the last year or more of his time in China, as shown in the chronological summary, affords a rough indication of the way in which he had to husband his strength in order to continue his ministry. Increasingly he had to withdraw to one or other of the Mission's health resorts, to Chefoo, or Kuling, or Mokanshan, that he might battle through.

His last long journey in China, during the days of his active service, was taken in company with the Rev. and Mrs. Charles Inwood, that he might be present at the important missionary conference at Chungking, when far-reaching decisions as to mission comity were made.

That gathering was in January 1899, and in September of the same year, after having spent the summer in the hills, he and Mrs. Taylor left China for a visit to Australia, New Zealand, and America. Mrs. Taylor was never to see China again, and Hudson Taylor only for a short seven weeks, five and a half years later. It was the beginning of the end in their lifelong journey. The years so full of strenuous activity were to be exchanged for years of quiet watching and waiting, and for the supreme trial of standing aside—and that from a work they had begotten, and for which they had travailed in labours and prayers.

It was while he was in America in the spring of 1900, after his last visit to Australasia, that the first serious signs of a breakdown manifested themselves. Dr. A. T. Pierson, with whom he was holding meetings in Boston, has recorded how, "in an otherwise effective address, he repeated one or two sentences a score of times or more." These sentences were:

> "You may trust the Lord too little, but you can never trust Him too much.
>
> "'If we believe not, yet He abideth faithful; He cannot deny himself.'"

"There was," continued Dr. Pierson, "something pathetic and poetic in the very fact that this repetition was the first visible sign of his breakdown, for was it not this very sentiment and this very quotation, that he had kept repeating to himself, and to all his fellow-workers during all the years of his missionary work? a blessed sentence to break down upon, which had been the buttress of his whole life of consecrated endeavour."

And we cannot perhaps do better than close this chapter with a few quotations from his addresses given during these last days of his active ministry, addresses given at the New York conference, and on other public occasions. They are the deliberate testimony of a man of God, given at the close of a life brim-full of crucial experiences, and as such are his matured convictions.

When he had sailed for China in 1853 there were only three hundred Chinese Christians in the whole of the Chinese Empire; when he spoke the words that follow there were 100,000 communicants in connection with the Protestant Churches, and no fewer than 25,000 Chinese had been baptized by the Mission God had used him to found. When he had first reached China a missionary might never be absent from a treaty port for more than twenty-four hours, under pain of deportation; but now the land was open from end to end for travel and residence. In his sayings there is a body of wisdom on practical matters pertaining to the spiritual life not easily equalled. Reference here can only be made to one or two. And first, in regard to the power of self-emptying and unresisting suffering, he said:

"We have tried to do, many of us, as much good as we felt we could easily do, or conveniently do, but there is a wonderful power when the love of God in the heart raises us to this point that we are ready to suffer, and with Paul we desire to know Him in the power of His resurrection (which implies the death of self), and the fellowship of His sufferings, being made conformable unto His death. It is ever true that what costs little is worth little....

"It is a serious and difficult problem very frequently, to know how far we should look to and accept the protection of our Governments, or their vindication, in case of riot and difficulty. I have seen both plans tried. I have never seen the plan in the long run successful, of demanding help and vindication from man. Wherever I have traced the result, in the long run there has been more harm done than good, and I have never seen the willingness to suffer and leave God to vindicate His own cause, His own people and their right, where the result has not been beneficial, if there has been rest and faith in Him; and praise God, I have known a number of such instances in the mission field."

On more than one occasion Hudson Taylor, during this time in America, made some striking remarks on the subject of sudden conversions which are well worth recording. Speaking at the New York conference, he stated that he had personally known at least one hundred Chinese who had accepted Christ as Saviour the first time they had ever heard of Him. On another occasion he gave the following arresting testimony on this important topic:

> "When I first went to China I expected people to be saved very soon, and before I could speak any Chinese at all God was pleased to give me the joy of seeing two accept Christ. By the time that year was over I had been so much under the influence of older and wiser men, who thought that a very gradual process of education was necessary before the heathen could be expected to become Christians, that I had ceased to expect instantaneous conversions; and for two or three years I was not disappointed, for I did not see any."

He then records a conversation held with a missionary recently come from England, which friend answered his arguments in favour of a slow preparation by saying: "I should not like to hold views like that, it seems perilously like sinning against the Holy Ghost."

> "Then I remembered," continued Hudson Taylor, "that my own conversion had been like a flash of fire; and I felt that I was wrong, and confessed the sin; and we went out together.... Well, I think it was in July my friend spoke to me in this way. On Christmas Day we had seven converted Christians meet together to spend a happy day. The Lord had blessed us to the conversion of seven!"

These closing discourses bring the reader into a wealthy country. They are full of quiet, simple, but mature convictions on many topics, on faith, on prayer, on the inspiration of God's Word, and on the faithfulness of God

Himself. It was out of the abundance of his heart, and out of the riches of his own experience, that he spoke. And this was the secret of his fruit-fulness. "It is a specially sweet part of God's dealings with His messengers," he once said, "that He always gives us the message for ourselves first.... He does not send us out with sealed despatches."

XXVI

UNTO THE LORD

O N JUNE 18, 1900, Mr. and Mrs. Hudson Taylor reached England from America. So critical was Hudson Taylor's condition that he was taken, without any delay, on to Switzerland, in order to secure freedom from all responsibility, and to obtain, if possible, restoration for further service. But this was not to be. Both he and Mrs. Taylor were passing into "the corridor of life's eventide." And that corridor was to be, for such active workers, somewhat long and trying. Mrs. Taylor was to be spared for four years, and Hudson Taylor for five years, before the final call came. But both could say: "Whether we live, we live unto the Lord; or whether we die, we die unto the Lord." Every possible experience that life could bring was covered by that attitude to God. "Whether we live or die, we are the Lord's."

There is something powerfully affecting in the sudden death of a warrior stricken down in the midst of the battle. But it is a far more searching test to character and faith to be laid aside in the midst of the conflict, and compelled to be a helpless spectator at a moment of critical importance. And this was to be Hudson Taylor's supreme trial.

We have mentioned that he reached England on June 18, 1900. During the twelve remaining days of that same month, no fewer than twelve missionaries, of his own beloved Mission, were to be cruelly done to

213

death in China. Thirty more suffered violent deaths in July, twelve more
in August, two more during September, and another two during October.
And these figures do not include twenty-one missionaries' children, which
brought the number of violent deaths, within the ranks of the China
Inland Mission alone, to the terrible total of seventy-nine. And beyond
this were the sad losses of other Societies, and the unnumbered martyrs
of the Chinese Church. For Hudson Taylor, the Father of his missionary
family—for such he was—to be laid aside at such an hour was discipline
indeed. He had always been in the vanguard of every movement, in the
forefront of every battle, at hand in every hour of danger, and now —to
be incapacitated, to be laid aside, and to be unable, in person, even to
soothe and sympathize with his fellow-soldiers and fellow-sufferers, was
the sorest trial that God's hand had permitted.

Never was his "soul more bent to serve" his Maker, to adopt some stately
words of Milton, written in his blindness. Milton wrote, and Hudson
Taylor believed, that:

> Who best
> Bear His mild yoke, they serve Him best. His state
> Is Kingly; thousands at His bidding speed.
> And post o'er land and ocean without rest;
> They also serve who only stand and wait."

How gladly would he have sped o'er land and ocean without rest! But to
"stand and wait" was what God asked of him; and it was, perhaps, a greater
service to the work he loved than he was able at that juncture to realize.
Though active responsibility had to be some-what suddenly transferred to
another, he was still spared for consultation, he was still alive to inspire
confidence among the friends of the Mission. The organization of the work
he had founded was practically complete. In the Home countries there
were Directors, Secretaries, and Councils; and in China itself there was
a Deputy Director and a China Council also. It only remained for him
to pass on to the tried and trusted hands of Mr. D. E. Hoste the responsibilities attaching to the post of General Director, first as acting on his
behalf, then, when recovery of health was clearly not God's Will, the full

commission as his successor, while he remained as Consulting Director. In this way, the work that he had founded passed, without a shock, to those whom God was raising up to take his place.

Happily, under God, the foundations of the Mission had been well and soundly laid, and he was able to write, in reply to a letter of loving sympathy signed by some three hundred members of the Mission, who had been driven from their stations by the Boxer persecutions, the following reassuring words:

> "When the resumption of our work in the interior becomes possible we may find circumstances changed, but the principles we have proved, being founded on God's unchanging Word, will be as applicable as ever."

How true those words were was not only proved after the Boxer crisis, but is being proved to-day, after the even more revolutionary upheaval of recent times. The rains have descended, the floods have come, the winds have blown, and beaten upon the house that he established, but, thank God, it has not fallen, for it was established upon the Rock.

The spirit in which he had built, and the spirit in which he transmitted his work to others, may be shown by a few words, taken from the last important official document he left when finally laying down his great responsibilities.

> "If," he wrote, "the Directors and Members of the Councils are godly and wise men, walking in the spirit of unity and love, they will not lack Divine guidance in important matters, and at critical times; but should another spirit prevail, no rules can save the Mission, nor would it be worth saving. The China Inland Mission must be a living body in fellowship with God, or it will be of no further use, and cannot continue."

As the months came and went, and the years passed by, it was not always easy to live that life of quiet and seclusion, especially after having been for so long in the thick of the fight. "It is hardest of all to do *nothing* for His sake," he once confessed; and at times the tears would stand in his eyes, though he was still prepared for all God's Will, whether it was to live unto the Lord, or die unto Him.

Exercised one day about the comparative comfort and leisure they were enjoying, Mr. and Mrs. Taylor found consolation in that day's message in *Daily Light:* "My people shall abide in a peaceful habitation, and in sure dwellings, and in quiet resting places." And so they gladly accepted what the Lord sent. And so Hudson Taylor rejoiced in the beauty of the flowers by day, and in the glory of the stars by night. He had always been a lover of Nature, and a pair of powerful binoculars, in lieu of a telescope, made the study of the heavens more delightful. Like the Psalmist who links the works and word of God together, Hudson Taylor did the same. To him the heavens declared the glory of God, and to him God's word was more to be desired than gold, yea, than much fine gold. And it was during these months in Switzerland that he, for the fortieth time in forty years, completed the reading of the whole Bible from *Genesis* to *Revelation.*

In 1903, the year in which he celebrated the jubilee of his first sailing for China, Mrs. Taylor manifested signs of that physical infirmity from which she died about a year later. Her mother had died of cancer, and she herself was stricken with the same dread disease, though mercifully neither she nor Mr. Taylor knew the real facts. It was a case in which surgical skill could do nothing, and the loved patient learned, in the quiet of her own room, "the lessons of the sweet power of helplessness and dependence," to quote her own words. And one of her joys, during those closing months, was to disburse, to various good causes, a legacy received from an uncle in Australia.

After a time of slowly ebbing strength, the end came quietly, on July 30, 1904, without, thank God, a long and painful period of suffering. And in the churchyard of La Chiesaz, not far from the pension at Chavelleyres, where they had been living, on the hills above the Lake of Geneva, she was laid to rest in the sure and certain hope of the Resurrection.

And now, the last long lonely reach of road lay before Hudson Taylor. The autumn was spent in the same lovely spot on the mountain side above the lake, the writer's sister—a trained nurse—being his companion. But in the winter a longing seized him to see once more the land of his adoption, and, as his health had substantially improved, this did not seem impossible. And so, in the company of his son and daughter-in-law, Dr. and Mrs. Howard Taylor, he set sail, on February 15, 1905, for what was to be his seventh visit to the United States of America, and his eleventh and last journey from England to China.

Shanghai was reached on April 17, 1905, and what a welcome he received, and how different from his first arrival there fifty-one years before! And what a contrast the following nearly seven weeks in China were to be, compared with his reception in 1854! Then he had been a stranger among strangers, and had been looked upon as an obscure missionary adventurer who was violating all recognized precedents. Now, he was an honoured veteran, whose faith in God, and whose wisdom in administration, commanded men's esteem. He had awakened a new enthusiasm in the whole mission-ary cause both at home and abroad, he had inspired men to attempt great things by the force of his own creative convictions, and had helped to raise the level of faith in God in the lives and experience of multitudes.

The weeks that followed were little short of a triumphal procession; both foreigners and Chinese alike rejoicing to do him reverence. Easter was spent at Yangchow, that scene of the riot thirty-seven years before. And God's acre at Chinkiang, where his first wife and four beloved children lay buried—and where he himself was laid to rest a few weeks hence—was visited. Three and a half weeks were spent in Honan, where the Chinese Christians vied with one another in showing their love, and here banners were presented to him inscribed with such tributes as: *Inland China's Benefactor,* or, *O Man greatly beloved,* the latter one being presented on Sunday, 21st May, his seventy-third birthday.

Hankow was reached on the thirty-ninth anniversary of the sailing of the *Lammermuir,* and from thence the party set sail, by river steamer, for Changsha, the capital of Hunan. For how many years had he prayed for this province, the last citadel of all that was anti-foreign and anti-Christian! And now he was to see it, and to see the accomplishment of his life-long desire, namely, the missionary occupation of the last province of China to be opened to the Gospel. And here he was to render up his spirit to God who gave it.

It was Thursday afternoon, the first of June, when Changsha was reached. Friday was spent in rest and in visiting parts of this famous city, including the site for the new hospital. On Saturday morning he spoke to the Chinese Christians assembled in the Chapel; in the afternoon he was present at a reception, given in the garden, to the missionary community of the city; and in the evening, after twilight had fallen, "in less time than it takes to write it," he was granted a swift entry into life immortal. The weary, worn-out warrior had found rest. And the translation was so sudden that it hardly seemed like death. He was not, for God took him.

And how wonderful, even dramatic, it all seemed! There could have been no more fitting spot in the whole world where he should breathe his last than in Changsha, the capital of the province which had been the last, and most resolute, in resisting the entrance of the Gospel. That he should finish his course there, represented, in splendid outline at least, the idea for which he had given his life, and for which he had built up the China Inland Mission. And it was as beautiful as it was becoming that the Hunan Christians should insist on providing the coffin for this Apostle of China. They had hoped that his dust might have been mingled with the soil of their province, but as his grave was to be at Chinkiang, beside his beloved wife and children, they would take no refusal in the matter of providing the best casket that could be purchased in the city.

In the English cemetery at Chinkiang, beside his dear ones, at the foot of the green hills near to the mighty Yangtse, the mortal remains of Hudson Taylor were laid to rest a few days later. It was there he had entered deeply into the fellowship of Christ in suffering, it was there he had learned the sufficiency of God's Unfailing Springs, and it is there he sleeps in Jesus till He come.

It has been said of one who died upon the heights of Mount Everest, higher than any other man has climbed, that "he was always drawn to the big and the unexplored—to the great walls that mountaineers, as a rule, set aside as obviously impossible. And while he climbed his eye was always on the watch for some fresh clue or hint that might give away the secret of their invincibility." And so it was with Hudson Taylor. The great things, the unachieved, the unevangelized regions drew him, and they inspired him to attempt the seemingly impossible for God. And so he laboured, and so he advanced, with his eye always on the watch for some fresh opportunity, some new opening, for some new adventure, that the strongholds of Satan might be captured for God, and that men might be brought into captivity to Jesus Christ.

To him there was "no dream that must not be dared;" no risk that must not be taken, if it came in the line of duty; no obstacle that could not be surmounted, if the call of God demanded. "Faith," he asserted, "laughs at impossibilities; and obedience raises no questions." And so, like Joshua and Caleb, undaunted by the fenced cities, and the sons of Anak, he wholly followed the Lord, and in His Name possessed the land.

If the secret of his life be asked, it is to be found in words already quoted; He believed in the Living God; he believed that God had spoken in His Holy Word; and he believed that God meant what He said, and would do all that He had promised.

NOT UNTO US BUT UNTO THY NAME

I F THERE is one thing more than another that Hudson Taylor would desire, it is that the last word should not be of man but of God, not of the servant but of the Master. By the grace of God he was what he was, and by the faithfulness of God he wrought what he did. As it is written: "He that glorieth, let him glory in the Lord."

And so we cannot bring this brief book to a better close than by leaving with the reader, as the last word, a beautiful passage from one of Hudson Taylor's little books, in which he ascribes all glory to Him who is the Giver of every good and perfect gift.

> "And what a glorious Father He is! the source of all true fatherhood and motherhood. We have often walked in the fields in the early morning, and have noticed how the rising sun has turned each dewdrop into a glittering gem; one ray of its own bright light making a little sun of each of the million drops that hang from the pendant leaflets and sparkle everywhere. But it is helpful to remember that the glorious orb itself contains infinitely more light than all the dewdrops ever did or ever will reflect. And so of our Heavenly Father: Himself the great Source of all that is noble and true, of all that ever has been loving and trustworthy—each beautiful trait of each beautiful character is but the dim reflection

of some ray of His own great perfection. And the sum-total of all human goodness, and tenderness, and love is but as the dewdrops to the sun. How blessed then to confide in the infinite and changeless love of such a Father—our Father in Heaven

"WHOSE FAITH FOLLOW."

APPENDIX

Dear Friend,

I feel that you, & all who aid us by your prayers, your sympathy, & your contributions, are partners with us in the great work laid upon our hearts — the evangelization of China.

J. Hudson Taylor.

A slightly reduced facsimile from one of Hudson Taylor's autograph letters.

CHRONOLOGICAL SUMMARY

1831-35.		Carl Gutzlaff's journeys up and down the China coast.
1832,	May 21.	J. Hudson Taylor born at Barnsley.
1834,	April 22.	East India Company's Trade monopoly ceases.
	August 1.	Robert Morrison dies at Canton.
1839,	November 3.	First Opium War commences.
1841,	January 20.	Hongkong ceded to the British.
1842,	August 29.	Treaty of Nanking signed.
1845.		Hue and Gabet visit Lhasa.
1850-64.		Taiping Rebellion.
1853,	March 19.	Taipings capture Nanking.
	September 7.	Triads capture Shanghai.
	September 19.	Hudson Taylor sails for China for the first time.
1854,	March 1.	Hudson Taylor lands in Shanghai.
1855-73.		Great Mohammedan rebellion in Yunnan.
1856-60.		Second Opium War.
1857,	June.	Hudson Taylor resigns from Chinese Evangelization Society.
1858,	January 20.	Hudson Taylor marries Miss Maria Dyer.
	June.	Treaty of Tientsin signed.
1860,	January 16.	Hudson Taylor's first appeal for helpers.
	July.	Mr. and Mrs. Hudson Taylor sail for England.

227

	October 24.	Treaty of Tientsin ratified at Peking.
1862-76.		Great Mahommedan rebellion in Kansu, etc.
1862,	January 8.	Hudson Taylor's first helpers, Mr. and Mrs. Meadows, sail.
1865,	April.	Three more workers sail for China.
	June 25.	Hudson Taylor's crisis at Brighton.
	October.	China's Spiritual Need and Claims published.
1866,	March 12.	Occasional Papers, No. 1 published.
	May 26.	Hudson Taylor sails for China, the second time, with Lammermuir party.
1867,	August 23.	Death of Gracie Taylor.
1868,	August 22-3.	Yangchow riot.
1869,	September 4.	Hudson Taylor's personal Pentecost.
	September.	Bitter anti-Christian manifesto issued from Hunan.
	November 17.	Suez Canal opened.
1870,	June 21.	Tientsin massacre.
	July 23.	Mrs. Hudson Taylor (nee Dyer) dies.
	August 24.	Nanking Viceroy assassinated.
1871,	June 3.	Telegraph cable opened to Shanghai.
	August.	Hudson Taylor sails for England.
	November 28.	Hudson Taylor marries Miss Faulding.
1872,	October 9.	Hudson Taylor sails for China, the third time, with Mrs. Taylor.
1874,	May.	Hudson Taylor falls and hurts spine.
	July 25.	Miss Blatchley dies.
	October 14.	Mr. and Mrs. Taylor reach England.
1875,	January.	Hudson Taylor's appeal for eighteen workers published.
	February 21.	Margary murdered.
	July.	China's Millions first published.
1876.		Beginning of Great Shansi Famine.
	September 7.	Hudson Taylor sails for China, the fourth time, without Mrs. Taylor, but with party of lady workers.
	September 13.	Chefoo Convention signed.
1877,	February 8.	First Chinese Envoy to London presents credentials.
	May 10-22.	General Missionary Conference at Shanghai.
	November.	Hudson Taylor sails for England.
1878,	May 2.	Mrs. Hudson Taylor sails for China, for famine relief work.

	August.	Hudson Taylor in Switzerland.
1879,	February 24.	Hudson Taylor sails for China, the fifth time.
	May 8.	Mr. and Mrs. Taylor reach Chefoo.
1880,	August.	Hudson Taylor's first visit to Kwangsin River.
1881,	October.	Mrs. Hudson Taylor sails for England; absent from China nine years.
	November.	Hudson Taylor at Wuchang. Appeal for The Seventy.
	December 10.	Hudson Taylor welcomes his eldest son, Herbert, to China.
1883,	February.	Hudson Taylor sails for England.
1885,	January 20.	Hudson Taylor sails, without Mrs. Taylor, for China, the sixth time.
	February 5.	The Cambridge Seven leave for China.
1886,	May-June.	Hudson Taylor's second visit to Kwangsin River.
	May-October.	Hudson Taylor's travels, visiting nine provinces.
	August 6.	Pastor Hsi set apart by Hudson Taylor.
	Nov. 13-26.	First meeting of China Council. Appeal for The Hundred.
1887,	January.	Hudson Taylor sails for England.
		Sailing of the Hundred.
		Marquis Tseng issues China: The Sleep and the Awakening.
1888,	June 23.	Hudson Taylor, with his son. Dr. Howard Taylor, sails for North America.
	October 5.	Hudson Taylor sails from Vancouver for China, the seventh time, with first North American contingent.
1889,	May 21.	Hudson Taylor arrives in England.
	July.	Hudson Taylor pays second visit to North America.
	October.	Hudson Taylor issues To Every Creature.
	November.	Hudson Taylor visits Sweden, Norway, and Denmark.
1890,	February 18.	New C.I.M. premises in Shanghai opened.
	March.	Hudson Taylor sails for China for eighth time, without Mrs. Taylor.
	April 29.	First Australian worker for C.I.M. arrives in Shanghai.
	May 7-20.	General Missionary Conference in Shanghai; Hudson Taylor preaches the opening sermon.
	June.	Formation of German China Alliance.
	August.	Hudson Taylor visits Australia for first time.
	November 20.	Hudson Taylor sails for China with first Australasian party.
	December 21.	Hudson Taylor reaches Shanghai, finds Mrs. Taylor there after an absence of nine years from China.

1891,	January.	Sailing of first Scandinavian China Alliance party. Many anti-foreign riots this year.
1892,	March.	Hudson Taylor reaches Vancouver. Ill.
	July 26.	Hudson Taylor arrives in England; visits Keswick. Ill.
1893,	April.	Hudson Taylor visits Germany.
	August.	Hudson Taylor visits Germany again.
1894,	February 14.	Hudson Taylor sails for China, the ninth time, via America, with Mrs. Taylor, and Miss Geraldine Guinness.
	February 14.	Hudson Taylor speaks at Students' Conference in Detroit.
	April 17.	Hudson Taylor reaches Shanghai.
	June.	Chinese and Japanese troops land in Korea. War follows.
	Summer.	Hudson Taylor takes long journey through heart of China.
1895,	April 17.	Treaty of Shimonoseki closes Chino-Japanese War.
	May.	Beginning of Szechwan riots.
	August 1.	Kucheng massacre.
	October 18.	Rev. W. W. Cassels consecrated as Bishop in Western China.
1896,	February.	Hudson Taylor, with Mrs. Taylor, leaves China. Ill.
	March.	Hudson Taylor visits India.
	April.	Hudson Taylor returns to China.
	May 2.	Hudson Taylor sails for England, lands at Brindisi and visits Germany en route.
	August.	Hudson Taylor visits Sweden, Norway and Germany.
1897,	early.	Hudson Taylor visits Mr. Berger in South France.
	Spring.	Hudson Taylor visits Germany.
	Summer.	Mr. and Mrs. Taylor, with Miss Williamson, in Switzerland.
	November 1.	Two German missionaries murdered in Shantung.
	November 1.	German troops occupy Kiaochow.
	November 24.	Hudson Taylor sails, via America, for China, the tenth time, with Mrs. Taylor, Miss Soltau and Miss Hanbury.
1898,	January 15.	Hudson Taylor reaches Shanghai, resides there three months.
	March 27.	Russia secures Port Arthur.
	April 10.	France claims Kwangchow-wan.
	April 20.	Hudson Taylor visits Chefoo.
	May 9.	Hudson Taylor back in Shanghai.
	Summer.	Hudson Taylor at Kuling.
	June.	Yli Mantze rebellion begins in Szechwan.

	July 1.	British obtain lease of Weihaiwei.
	September 22.	Coup d'etat. Empress Dowager resumes power in Peking.
	October.	Hudson Taylor back in Shanghai.
	November 4.	Murder of Mr. Fleming in Kweichow.
	November.	Mr. and Mrs. Taylor, with Mr. and Mrs. Inwood, start for West China Conference.
1899,	January 16-21.	Conference in Chungking; 80 persons present.
	March 15.	Official status given to Roman Catholic missionaries.
	April 6.	Hudson Taylor back in Shanghai.
	May 24.	Hudson Taylor visits Chefoo, for the last time. Hudson Taylor back in Shanghai for Council Meetings.
	July 18.	Hudson Taylor goes to Mokanshan for summer. The Boxer Society founded this summer. Many riots.
	September 1.	Hudson Taylor back in Shanghai for last days of active service in China.
	September 26.	Mr. and Mrs. Taylor leave China for Australia and New Zealand. Close of Hudson Taylor's work in China.
	November 21.	Empress Dowager issues her famous anti-foreign decree.
	December 31.	Mr. S. M. Brooks murdered in Shantung.
1900,	January.	Mr. and Mrs. Taylor, with Dr. and Mrs. Howard Taylor, visit New Zealand.
	April.	Hudson Taylor at New York Ecumenical Missionary Conference.
	May.	Boxer outbreaks begin.
	June 18.	Mr. and Mrs. Taylor reach England, and proceed to Switzerland.
	June 24.	Imperial Decree orders murder of all foreigners.
1904,	July 30.	Mrs. Hudson Taylor dies in Switzerland.
1905,	February 15.	Hudson Taylor sails for China for the last time.
1905,	June 3.	Hudson Taylor dies at Changsha, Hunan.

INDEX

SCRIPTURE TESTIMONY INDEX

After his conversion, Hudson Taylor went to commune with God in prayer and there asked to be used of Him. Taylor had an "unutterably real and blessed" experience of God's presence, and the conviction that God had called him to China.

Hudson Taylor was blessed with godly parents, who not only dedicated him to the Master even before his birth, but raised him up in the way of Lord, laying the necessary foundation upon which Hudson would eventually stand; going on to influence millions for the Kingdom of God through the China Inland Mission.

Fifteen-year-old Hudson Taylor had picked up a little gospel tract to read, simply as a diversion. But at that same time, several miles away, his mother felt led to pray to God for his conversion. Locking her door, she cried for hours until she could no longer pray, but instead thanked God for answering her prayer. Indeed, her timely prayer was answered!

An older minister tried to discourage Hudson Taylor from having a child-like faith in God as it pertained to his call to China, reasoning that the days of trusting God for provision had long passed. Many years later, Taylor was able, from his rich experience, to reaffirm his childlike confidence in the promises of God.

In obedience to the heavenly vision and call to go to China, Hudson Taylor, like a workman not wanting to be put to shame, devoted himself to careful study of Chinese, Greek, Latin, theology and medicine. He also made changes in his habits to discipline his flesh. All these things he did to prepare himself for his life's work.

Hudson Taylor was asked to pray for a sick woman. He found the woman and her family to be in a truly wretched condition, and in great need. Yet all Taylor had was his very last half-crown piece. He tried to pray but could not while that coin remained in his pocket. When the husband finally asked for his help, the scripture, "Give to him that asketh of thee" flashed across his mind. Taylor obeyed, saving the woman's life and conquering self as a result.

Hudson Taylor was robbed and abandoned by his own servant on his way to Ningpo to get medical supplies. But in spite of this and the resulting weariness and hunger, he was more concerned about preaching Christ Jesus to the unbelievers around.

Hudson Taylor had to destroy the clothing he had been wearing while nursing a friend stricken with smallpox. That left him in need of clothes, but with no money to buy them. It was just at this juncture that Taylor's Heavenly Father stepped in to provide perfectly-timed help to His son.

Hudson Taylor ran out of money to supply free breakfast to a number of destitute people. But just then some money due to his colleague arrived earlier than expected, which met the very important need at hand.

In order to get money for food, for themselves, and the guests they were expecting, Hudson Taylor and Mr. Jones tried to sell some household possessions, but could not. Turning to God as their only hope, they cried for help. While they were still on their knees, He supplied a "rich relief!"

"Call upon Me in the day of trouble; I will deliver thee, and thou shalt glorify Me." Distraught Hudson Taylor heard these words as he sought a doctor in an effort to save his dying wife. In faith he obeyed and was instantly filled with peace—a peace beyond all understanding. On returning home from the doctor's, he found that the Great Physician Himself had visited his wife.

Dr. Parker's return to Scotland created a new need for the missionaries in China as the expenses incurred to run the hospital and dispensary were until that time, borne by him. But holding onto the promise to seek God's Kingdom first and have "all these things" added to them, they chose to trust and not to close down the hospital. God rewarded their faith.

So solid was his faith in his Heavenly Father and the His living word that Hudson Taylor declared, "God's work done in God's way will never lack God's supplies" His faith in the scriptures was unshakable and His experience as a father only helped solidify his belief that His Heavenly Father would never forget him.

Hudson Taylor was becoming sick with anxiety over the prospect of asking people to join him in the dangerous and difficult work in China. Only by fully trusting in God for his *own* welfare and direction did Hudson Taylor get peace to trust Him for the welfare and direction of future workers.

Hudson Taylor demonstrated in his life and ministry that "The meek do not possess by force, but, as children, by inheritance."

When unforeseen circumstances prevented a notice appealing for funds from going public, the amount needed was still secured in answer to prayer alone, causing a grateful Hudson Taylor to declare: "Truly, there is a living God, and He is the Hearer and Answerer of prayer."

For Hudson Taylor, identifying with the Chinese among who he worked, in all things not sinful: their culture, attire, architecture and so on, was following in the footsteps of Jesus who meekly left Heaven to be cradled in a manger so as to save humanity from sin and destruction.

Take the gospel to the ends of the earth................................... 119
Mark 16:15 · Acts 1:8 · Acts 6:7 · Colossians 1:23

In an audacious expression of faith in God and a literal obedience to the charge by Jesus to take the gospel to the ends of the earth, Hudson Taylor—in the company of 21 other believers—set out for China on Saturday, May 26, 1866. "They had no one at home to guarantee them support; they had no one in China to welcome them; they had no home ready to receive them." They had only their faith in Jesus Christ—and it was all they needed.

Believers are the aroma of Christ to those around them
2 Corinthians 2:14-16
Christians care for one another in love................................... 120
John 13:34-35 · 1 John 3:11-24

Hudson Taylor was gifted in the management of the class and cultural diversity among the pioneer missionaries travelling to China aboard the *Lammermuir* in 1866. His personal example and loving leadership were such that instead of personal conflicts among the missionaries, more than half of the crew members of the ship confessed Jesus as their Lord and Saviour before they even arrived in Shanghai.

Afflictions borne for the Gospel are light and momentary.......... 122
2 Corinthians 4:7-18

For Hudson Taylor and his missionary companions, reaching the many Chinese souls that were yet without a Saviour was of paramount importance. Every discomfort they had to suffer for that goal was welcomed. And so, with a smile rather than a complaint, hardships associated with their work were borne.

Our Father in heaven gives good things................................... 128
Matthew 7:9-11

Hudson Taylor shares how his great love for his children despite his failings, assures him that God, being a more loving Father than he could ever be, will never leave nor forsake him.

A blatantly false accusation of being responsible for the loss of twenty-two Chinese children was used by an enraged mob to lay siege to the missionary premises in Yangchow. Some of missionaries were badly stoned, and there was much injury to others as they tried to escape.

The Taylors were undaunted even after suffering intense persecution and trials. In separate letters, they both counted their suffering as light and momentary for the sake of gospel, fixing their eyes on the weightier eternal glory that a harvest of souls would bring to God's Kingdom.

After the sad loss of his dearest wife, Hudson Taylor did not go on grieving as one without hope. In total submission to the will of God, he believed that it was for the best—for her and for him—that she was called home to be with the Lord.

Hudson Taylor wrote to his sister about the abundant joy and peace that had replaced the great distress and restlessness that had burdened him for months because of a growing consciousness of his own sin and his powerlessness against it. When he found that Jesus had promised to never leave him and that he was literally a member of Christ's body, he was able to conclude, "Can Christ be rich and I poor?"

Hudson Taylor writes about the deep rest and fullness of life, that a knowledge of Christ's indwelling in him has brought him. Gladly he says, "Christ dwelling in the heart by faith... is power indeed, is life indeed."

Blessed are those who mourn 150
Matthew 5:4 · Luke 6:21

As Hudson Taylor mourned the loss of his dear wife and two sons, as well as the absence of the ones who were living. He writes beautifully about the deep comfort brought to him by the Lord during this difficult time. In Taylor's words, "No language can express what He has been and is to me... He who once wept at the grave of Lazarus often now weeps in and with me..."

Those who believe in Jesus shall be filled with the Spirit 151
John 4:10 · John 7:37-38

Like Jesus offered to the Samaritan woman, Hudson Taylor was able, in a moment of great need and thirst, access the well that never runs dry. No longer was the Samaritan woman's story ancient history to him, for in his own words, "it became a present message to my soul... and more than satisfied my sorrowing heart."

Ask Me anything in My name 159
Matthew 18:19 · John 14:13-14 · John 16:23-24

"Whatsoever ye shall ask in My Name, I will do it, that the Father may be glorified in the Son." This was the promise upon which Hudson Taylor rested with absolute certainty as the mission trusted God for a hundred new workers and the funds to meet their needs. And they were not disappointed, as God kept His promise.

For God so loved the world that He gave His only Son 187
John 3:16

Hudson Taylor's departure to China, and the loss of his little daughter there, helped him and his own mother to understand John 3:16 more fully... "God so loved the world that He gave His only son."

Spiritual burden for a lost people group to be saved 191
Romans 9:1-3

With great passion, Hudson Taylor burned for China and the many unsaved souls there. Not only did he offer himself to be used by God for the Chinese, but with illustrative stories and unwearied zeal, he appealed to fellow believers with the need to also burn for these unsaved souls.

Hudson Taylor shares two stories of believers going out of their way to support God's work in China as best they could, from a widowed woman giving away a prized possession for the sake of the work, to a young boy giving his entire savings.

Hudson Taylor understood that the church of God will always be a body with many members and he committed to promoting and supporting the work of other missionaries and members of the body. For him, the ultimate aim of winning souls was more important than any organizational or denominational difference.

Instead of with spite or bitterness, Hudson Taylor treated even the men with whom he disagreed with brotherly love. Rather than focus on areas of disagreement with others, he was focused on shared unity in Christ Jesus.

In 1886, a small group of believers from the China Inland Mission were gathered together to seek the face of God, and for eight days they offered prayers and fasted. The Lord honored His people as their petitions were granted.

Walking Together Press is a non-profit publishing
company devoted to supporting grassroots libraries in
Africa through global book sales and through
providing free library editions.

To read our story, to see our catalog, and to learn
more about how you can help us in our mission,
visit our website at:

https://walkingtogether.press